Offbeat New

Places of Unexpected History, Art, and Culture

Neala McCarten

Copyright: 2016 Neala McCarten
Neala@OffbeatTravel.com

ISBN-10:
0-9973322-1-2
ISBN-13:
978-0-9973322-1-6

All photographs by Neala McCarten
Cover photo taken at Petroglyph National Monument in Albuquerque
Cover Design by Barbara Rosen

I may have written this book alone, but I've had much help getting it to print and e-book status.

Author of the delightful Sam Darling murder mysteries, Jerilyn Dufresne helpfully suggested Polgarus Studios for the editing and formatting. Accessible travel writer Candy Harrington offered advice and suggestions about the publishing process. Betsy Model provided much appreciated suggestions and assistance. The online group HWW helped with cover selection and fine-tuning the title.

Thank you to my husband James McCarten for his support and encouragement.

And to those who no longer work this earth but who always believed I could accomplish whatever I set out to do – thank you. You have given me the courage to pursue my goals, and my dreams.

Note: There are numerous links in the book for your convenience, and further information. Each link was checked and they were accurate and working at the time the book was published. Unfortunately, links do change, and sometimes they go bad. We apologize for any inconvenience this might cause.

WHAT PEOPLE ARE SAYING ABOUT
OFFBEAT NEW MEXICO

"No matter how long you have lived in New Mexico or how many times you've visited the state, *Offbeat New Mexico* includes fascinating insider information about the Land of Enchantment that will surprise even the most experienced traveler."
    -- John W. Byram, The University of New Mexico Press

"*Offbeat New Mexico* is an indispensable guide to the most interesting places in Albuquerque, Taos, and Santa Fe, but its soul is in the small towns and open roads. Let Neala McCarten lead you to the treasures of the state: from the majesty of Ghost Ranch to a hardware store stuffed with taxidermy; from dinosaur fossils to Hatch chiles; from Smokey Bear's grave to the Classical Gas Museum. *Offbeat New Mexico* makes me want to hop on a plane, rent a convertible, and hit the blue highways of the Land of Enchantment."
    -- Dave Feldman, Author of the Imponderables (R) book series

"More than a guidebook, *Offbeat New Mexico* takes an in-depth look into the state's fascinating towns and amazing historical sites with surprising discoveries and intriguing insight. From Aztec's ancient Puebloan ruins and Roswell's mysterious UFO chronicles, to Georgia O' Keeffe's domicile in Ghost Ranch, *Offbeat New Mexico* provides an exciting palette of destinations to explore. A must read for any serious visitor or southwestern history enthusiast."
    -- Patrice Raplee, Editor for *Travel Excursion* & Radio Talk Show Correspondent

"Even New Mexicans don't know all there is to know about our enchanted state, but *Offbeat New Mexico* tells all. I found out about places I haven't visited, and facts I hadn't known about my adopted home. I'm giving a copy to every guest who rides in for Balloon Fiesta."
    -- Stephanie Hainsfurther, Publisher of two online magazines devoted to the arts in Albuquerque and the people of New Mexico.

PREFACE

I visited Albuquerque in 2004, and fell instantly in love. New Mexico is called the Land of Enchantment for a reason—it bewitches unwary visitors. I vowed to move to this wild, fascinating place of open lands, rich culture, and unexpected history.

Two years later I had sold my house, quit my job, said goodbye to my friends, and moved to Albuquerque. I have never looked back.

History had always been the epitome of boring when I was in school—an endless series of dates that had no meaning to me. My attitude toward history changed dramatically when I became a travel writer. Instead of reading a dry list of people and dates, I was standing in the places where history happened, places filled with stories. People were heroes and villains, sometimes both. They had past lives. Sometimes they had a future. Sometimes they did not. I became entranced by the stories of these places. When I moved to New Mexico my passion for history led me to explore the historic places of my new home.

The result is this book. It's not a travel guide. It won't tell you where to eat, or sleep. Sites like TripAdvisor and Yelp describe and evaluate restaurants and hotels. I see no need to duplicate their content.

Offbeat New Mexico is a guide through New Mexico's several hundred years of intriguing history. It was the Wild West until perhaps ... yesterday.

But Offbeat New Mexico could easily be a guide to the cultures that created this tri-cultural state, or to the art that begins with petroglyphs and ends up as street art on the walls of Albuquerque, or on the half-mile of art in Santa Fe known as Canyon Road.

Offbeat New Mexico is for readers who seek to understand the soul of a place and for travelers who want to explore the history, the art, the culture that is the complicated and unexpected richness of New Mexico. It is my chosen home, and I hope this book shares some of the fascination and passion that brought me here, to the Land of Enchantment.

Neala McCarten

TABLE OF CONTENTS

MEET NEW MEXICO

If there's one odd juxtaposition of statistics that sums up New Mexico, it's that the Land of Enchantment is the fifth biggest state in terms of square miles, but it only ranks thirty-sixth in population with just over two million people. Almost half of those people call the greater metropolitan area of Albuquerque home. That's a whole lot of land for the remaining population.

It is a land of the unexpected and unconventional. There are historical events and movements rarely found outside the state and a population that relishes the opportunity to go its own way, often creating new developments in art, science and the environment. Even the architecture is a fusion of styles. The best way to know New Mexico is through its places—where all that history, culture, art, and even quirk collide.

FROM CLOVIS MAN TO THE SPANISH CONQUEST AND THE BUFFALO SOLDIERS

New Mexico has had an extraordinary human history, which started over 12,000 years ago with the earliest prehistoric resident, Clovis Man, who was named after a distinctive arrowhead that was found near present-day Clovis in eastern New Mexico.

Next the ancient Puebloans (sometimes called the Anastasi) settled in the area around 1200 AD, and built their adobe communities in the northern part of the state. The ruins show the richness of their lives and their culture and have become both national and state parks and monuments.

Although people used to puzzle over what happened to them, the Native Americans of New Mexico find that reaction humorous, replying that the ancient Puebloans didn't disappear. Their descendants are found in the pueblos of New Mexico and in other Native American groups.

New Mexico is also home to the Navajo, whose land stretches across the Four Corners, where the states of Utah, Colorado, New Mexico, and Arizona meet.

THE SPANISH COME TO THE NEW WORLD

With the "discovery" of the new world, Spanish conquistadores came searching for the legendary Cities of Gold. Some of the routes they created still exist today, including El Camino Real (The Royal Road), a 1,200-mile trade route starting in Mexico City and ending in Santa Fe.

The conquest did not go smoothly. The people of the pueblos did not readily submit to Spanish domination and sought to maintain their traditional religious beliefs and practices. Moreover, the Spanish used their labor and took the products of that labor, maintaining their rule through terror. When the people of the pueblos had enough, they banded together and revolted. Generally known as the Pueblo Revolt of 1680, it is also known as Popé's (or Po'pay), Rebellion, after one of its major leaders.

The Spanish colonial era eventually ended, but there was still turmoil in the area. The settlers and the native peoples often clashed. Although the Navajo homeland included western New Mexico when settlers arrived, hostilities emerged that eventually led to the infamous "Long Walk" in the spring of 1864. Bands of Navajo were forced to relocate to Fort Sumner in an area called the Bosque Redondo. Eventually, the United States and Navajo leaders

> **Did You Know...**
>
> **When It Comes to Water No State Is Drier than New Mexico?**
>
> Although the state is large, it has very little surface water. The total surface water area is only 250 square miles. According to US Census Bureau data, only .02% of New Mexico's surface area is covered by water, making it the state with the least amount of surface water in the country given its size. Arizona is next with .03%. New Mexico is also one of the driest in the country in terms of precipitation.

signed a treaty at Fort Sumner on June 1, 1868 and the Navajo were given back their land.

In addition to their desire for colonization, the Spanish brought something else to the area: the Spanish Inquisition. Since the late 1300s, the church in Spain had sought to convert the Jews of Spain.

But by the mid-1400s there was growing concern that not all of the converted Jews were truly Christian. There was concern that some "converts" may even be practicing the banned religious rites in secrecy. Anyone determined not truly converted could be tortured until they confessed, then often killed afterward. Jews who refused to convert were forced from their homes and from Spanish lands.

This zeal to root out false conversions followed the Spanish to Mexico and then up to the lands of New Mexico, where numerous of these hidden or Crypto Jews had fled. In 1626, the Spanish Inquisition came to New Mexico. Its goal was to insure that the New Christians, as the converted Jews were called, did not revert to their old religious ways. The book To the End of the Earth by Stanley M. Hordes, former State Historian of New Mexico, is an excellent exploration of the topic. One place in New Mexico has been officially identified as a part of the Inquisition: the site Quarai of the Salinas Pueblo Missions National Monument near Mountair.

In 1850, New Mexico became a United States territory. It became the forty-seventh state in 1912.

BUFFALO SOLDIERS

You'll find the history of the Buffalo Soldiers at several forts throughout the state. Black cavalry and infantry troops had fought in the Civil War, but when that war ended there was serious opposition to the Black soldiers serving in the peacetime military.

There was still plenty of fighting, however. The area that is now New Mexico and Texas needed soldiers to staff the forts during the Indian Wars and protect the settlers, miners, and the trails that brought commerce through the area. In 1866, eight Black companies of the 125th Infantry marched to New Mexico. They served at seven Army forts throughout the territory, most of them in southern New Mexico.

The Kiowa tribe is said to have given the Buffalo Soldiers their name as homage to the admired qualities of courage and fortitude of the soldiers. Taken as a compliment by the troops, the 10th Cavalry adopted a picture of the buffalo as its regiment crest.

In 1997, the movie Buffalo Soldiers depicted the all-black US Cavalry Troop H and its attempts to capture an Apache warrior named Vittorio who slaughters the settlers in New Mexico. Watch the trailer for the movie at: https://youtu.be/Om_BrJhu4gQ

By the 1890s, the hostilities ceased and the forts closed. The Buffalo Soldiers had fulfilled their mission. The oldest Buffalo Soldier, Mark Matthews, died on September 6, 2005. He is interred at Arlington National Cemetery. He was 111 years old.

COMMERCE DRIVES NEW MEXICO: THE SANTA FE TRAIL, THE IRON HORSE, FRED HARVEY, AND ARCHITECTURE

Although it was not part of the developed East or Midwest, New Mexico still participated in commerce. In the 1800s, the famous Santa Fe Trail became a commercial highway connecting Missouri with Santa Fe. But that other earlier trail, El Camino Real (the Royal Road), connected Santa Fe with Mexico, thus creating a trade route bringing goods from Mexico City to El Paso and into New Mexico and Santa Fe, then through to Missouri.

That system worked well until it was eclipsed by the iron horse. In 1879, the railroad came to New Mexico with the arrival of the legendary Atchison, Topeka, and Santa Fe Railroad line (AT&SF), which, despite its name, never actually came to Santa Fe. Instead, the famous line ended in Lamy, New Mexico and used a spur line into the capital city.

The railroad was a powerful economic engine, driving development across the state. Its arrival made towns instantly successful, connecting them to this new commercial highway. But when the railroad left, many of the towns died. Today they make up some of the ghost towns strewn across the state. The railroad did more than bring goods, though. It also brought tourists eager to experience Native American culture and the wonders of the Wild West.

Originally, the railway stops were quite crude. The train would pause at a depot for a few minutes while passengers frantically scrambled for food. Fred Harvey saw a need and filled it with hotels, restaurants, and gift shops, aptly named Harvey Houses, and staffed them with Harvey Girls. He changed the railway experience to one of comfort and commerce.

The buildings were architectural gems, and they offered a collection of Native American arts and crafts available for purchase. Although most of that history has been demolished, some pieces still remain as cherished icons of a vanished era.

From the beginning New Mexico was a fertile land for architectural fusion. It started with the adobe structures of the pueblos and was leavened by Spanish influences. The railroad brought designs of the Midwest into the Southwest, and many examples still exist across the state, but three styles in particular are worth noting.

The design used in building the pueblos busted out of its Native American origins to become reimagined as Pueblo Revival, possibly the most popular style for residential housing. In its purest form it is angular and boxy. Roofs are flat. Inside there are often vigas (huge wooden beams that cross the ceilings of adobe buildings) and latillas (small logs laid between vigas, often in a herringbone pattern) found in pueblo architecture. The buildings are covered in genuine adobe, or a stucco coating reminiscent of adobe. The floors inside are usually tiled or brick. There's almost always a kiva fireplace—the round adobe hearth that becomes a focal point in the room.

Territorial style became popular as New Mexico transitioned from a territory to a state. It's a hybrid influenced by Greek Revival that became the rage. Its key elements include flat roofs and white-painted wood lintels over doors and windows to accent the existing adobe brick walls. Bricks atop exterior walls helped protect the fragile adobe from water damage.

The state was also home to examples of a style known as Pueblo Deco. This wonderfully flamboyant (but sadly short-lived) architectural style was popular in the Southwest. It fused aspects of the Native American culture with the distinctive geometrical design of Art Deco.

GETTING THEIR KICKS ON ROUTE 66 AND THE ATOMIC BOMB

When America took to the automobile, New Mexico benefited again. Route 66, established in 1926, was the Main Street of America—the Mother Road linking cities and towns across the country. The towns along the route built hotels and shops, gas stations, and roadside attractions to house, feed, and amuse visitors. Today these towns are in various states of restoration or decline, adding another layer to the ghost town history of the state.

But there were still other economic revolutions. Coal, gold, silver, turquoise, oil, gas, and more were found and more towns sprung up to mine the treasure. Even uranium was found in abundance—although that has proved to be a mixed blessing. As with every other economic revolution in the state, when the mines went bust it left more towns disintegrating in the sun, wind, and heat of the desert.

The coming of World War II was of major significance for New Mexico history. The town of Los Alamos was created for scientists, and military bases were developed across the state. The testing of the atomic bomb happened at Trinity site. The White Sands Missile Range is still in existence. There were even prisoner-of-war camps constructed (although little of these remain).

A VIBRANT TRI-CULTURAL STATE FILLED WITH FASCINATING HISTORY AND INCREDIBLE NATURAL BEAUTY

The result of this long and varied history is a tri-cultural state with the rich traditions of the Native Americans, the Spanish, and the Anglo inhabitants.

The history of the wars that were fought here can be found in our forts. Crops have been grown and festivals created. Arts have flourished. There are historic churches in almost every town.

It is a land of contrasts, from the hot deserts of the south to the wooded mountains of the north. There are remains of the ancestral Puebloans and the still living culture of their descendants. Visitors can explore Spanish colonial history as well as atomic bomb history. Take one of the scenic roads, tour state parks that make our natural beauty accessible, or disappear into the backcountry for hiking or mountain climbing.

New Mexico's boomtown legacy has left historic theaters in small towns across the state. Many are undergoing revitalization such as the Luna Theater in Clayton, the Shuler Theater in Raton, as well as the stellar KiMo Theater in Albuquerque.

Today, New Mexico is still evolving. Craft breweries fill our small towns and big cities, and our inner creativity is fueling innovation in our spirits-ual growth (rum, gin, whiskey).

Bring your camera when you explore New Mexico and you'll bring home memories you won't find elsewhere.

You'll drive by descansos (roadside memorials). You'll be asked the state's official question: Red or Green? This actually refers to whether you want your chile to be red or green. You'll see biscochitos for sale—the state cookie. Yes, there's a state cookie. Why not? We have a state tie (it's the bolo) and a state bird —our odd semi-flightless bird, the roadrunner. Just to make sure visitors understand that New Mexico is not like other places, the state capital Santa Fe has the nickname The City Different.

NEW MEXICO: TOWNS AND CITIES

New Mexico is usually divided up into six regions, each with its own distinctive history, landscape, and attractions.

NORTHWEST

This area of the state is known for its Native American heritage. It has a significant Navajo influence as well as vibrant Pueblo culture.

ACOMA PUEBLO (SEE ALSO GRANTS-MILAN)

The Acoma Pueblo, known as Sky City for its lofty perch high above the land below, offers stunning panoramic views of the surrounding sandstone bluffs and multihued mesas. The only way to visit the pueblo is by a guided tour—and you'd want to do that anyway. The tour provides a fascinating look at Pueblo life, both past and present. The museum presents a close look at the pottery, weaving, and artisan crafts of the living Pueblo culture.

The tour starts at the **Acoma Pueblo's Sky City Cultural Center and Haak'u Museum**, brilliantly designed to evoke a sense of the architecture and cultural heritage of the Acoma people. It is a beautiful setting that showcases their art and culture from their traditional handmade pottery to their distinctive jewelry. If you get hungry, the museum has a restaurant that specializes in Pueblo-inspired dishes.

The Acoma Pueblo covers about 75 acres atop a 357-foot-high sandstone mesa that overlooks the valley floor. The legendary Sky City is one of the oldest continuously inhabited settlements in the United States (Taos Pueblo is the other).

One of the tour highlights is a visit to the pueblo's 375-year-old San Esteban del Rey Mission, with its unique fusion of

Christianity and traditional Native American religious symbols.

There is no specified address, but the website offers a map.
(800) 747-0181
http://www.acomaskycity.org/home.html

The Acoma Pueblo was also one of the ignition points of the Pueblo Revolt of 1680, having experienced the exceedingly harsh punishment of the Spanish Colonial government.

SPECIAL FOCUS: PUEBLO REVOLT OF 1680—ALSO KNOWN AS POPÉ'S REBELLION

The origins of the conflict go back to 1598, when Juan de Onate conquered the region for Spain. The Spanish came to the area in search of the legendary Cities of Gold, but there were no golden cities. Instead, there were small Native American settlements that the Spanish called Pueblos—Little Towns.

Subsistence farmers and cultivators of the soil had little to offer the Spanish conquerors, but that didn't stop the Spanish from taking whatever they had. One of the earliest and most egregious examples of Spanish violence took place at the Acoma Pueblo. In 1599, Juan de Zaldivar took hostages in an attempt to extort flour and other supplies from the pueblo. The Acoma people revolted, killing de Zaldivar and 12 others. The Spanish, in turn, came down with draconian force, killing 800 and chopping one foot off surviving men over the age of 25. Men between the ages of 12 and 25 and women over the age of 12 were sentenced to 20 years of servitude.

The Spanish also felt they were on a divine mission to convert the heathens, but they could never totally quash the local religion. Governor Juan Trevino ordered the arrest and whipping of 47 shamans, ultimately killing four of them. Trevino, in turn, was taken hostage by 70 Pueblo warriors. In order to secure his freedom, he had to release the remaining 43 prisoners, including the man known as Popé (or Po'pay) leader of the Ohkay Owingeh Pueblo.

Under Popé's leadership, the Pueblos united to drive out the Spanish in 1680, killing 400 Spanish and driving 2,000 settlers out of the province. The victory was not permanent. Twelve years later in 1692, the Spanish returned and reconquered the Pueblos. A second revolt followed, but it was no more successful than the first one.

By the time the Spanish reconquest was complete, the politics of the region had shifted. Spain was more interested in New Mexico as a barrier territory between the French and Mexico's northern provinces. This meant that the forced labor program ended and that there was greater tolerance for the religious ceremonies of the Pueblos.

Read more here: http://newmexicohistory.org/people/pueblo-runners-and-the-pueblo-revolt-1680

AZTEC

It's not often you find historic ruins in the middle of a town, but that is exactly where you find the **Aztec Ruins National Monument**—located in downtown Aztec. The most notable part of the ruins is the reconstruction of the Great Kiva, which gives visitors a real sense of the kiva as a meeting place.

725 Ruins Road
Aztec, NM 87410
(505) 334-6174
http://www.nps.gov/azru/index.htm

Enjoy this NPS video created by Youth in Park Rangers that provides an overview of the ruins.
https://youtu.be/UCv8hVoaZ9I

BLOOMFIELD

Part of the Four Corners area, Bloomfield is known for its famous **Salmon Ruins**. In a way, the history of the ruins encapsulates the story of New Mexico. The first inhabitants were migrants from Chaco Canyon who built their dwellings there around 1090 AD. Although fire destroyed much of the site in the thirteenth century, that wasn't the end of the settlement. In the late nineteenth century, homesteaders Peter and George Salmon settled on the property. Remains of their cabin and outbuildings are preserved at the site. Salmon Ruins is listed on the US National Register of Historic Places and the New Mexico State Register of Cultural Properties.
6131 US-64
Bloomfield, NM 87413
(505) 632-2013
http://www.salmonruins.com

Chaco Canyon is famous for being a major center of ancestral Puebloan culture. It is considered to be one of the finest examples of the habitat-building skills of the peoples who lived in the area between 850 and 1250 AD. The park offers guided tours, hiking, and biking trails. There are 3,000 architectural structures on the grounds according to the National Park Service. From the Visitor Center, there is a nine-mile loop road that allows access to five major sites. Short self-guided trails are marked at each site.

This video made by the NPS Youth in Park Rangers introduces visitors to the wonders of Chaco.
https://youtu.be/xyiv9dV4UWg

Chaco is one of the more difficult parks to reach. Access requires driving on dirt roads. The NPS issues a warning about using your GPS to reach the park. Instead, they suggest visitors use these directions:
http://www.nps.gov/chcu/planyourvisit/directions.htm

CHURCH ROCK (SEE ALSO GALLUP)

The Navajo town of Church Rock, located about 10 miles east of Gallup, is named for its prominent natural landmark. The sandstone spire draws photographers seeking to capture the definitive image of the natural landmark. Church Rock is also sadly notorious for being the site of one of the worst nuclear breaches in United States history.

SPECIAL FOCUS: CHURCH ROCK NUCLEAR DISASTER

On July 16, 1979, the United Nuclear Corporation's Church Rock uranium mill tailings disposal pond broke through its dam. Over 1,000 tons of solid radioactive waste and 93 million gallons of acidic, radioactive tailings solution flowed into the Puerco River. Local residents used river water for irrigation and livestock and were not immediately told of the toxic danger. Contaminants then traveled 80 miles down the river into Arizona. The Navajo were never able to secure Superfund money for the cleanup.

The accident has been described as releasing more radioactivity than Three Mile Island and is considered to be the largest release of radioactive material in United States history.

This event goes a long way to explain Navajo reluctance to open their lands to uranium mining.

Read more about the consequences of the Church Rock disaster:
http://en.wikipedia.org/wiki/Church_Rock_uranium_mill_spill
http://www.latimes.com/news/la-na-navajo21nov21-story.html#page=3

CROWNPOINT (SEE ALSO GRANTS)

This largely Native American town is the site of the most important Navajo rug auction in New Mexico, the **Crownpoint Rug Auction**. The Crownpoint Rug Weavers Association holds the monthly auction in the town of Crownpoint, near Grants.

It's probably the best, and certainly the most fun, way to buy a Navajo rug. The auction brings in a couple hundred rugs from all over the Navajo Nation and almost that many bidders. Each area has its own distinctive style, embellished by the creativity of the weavers themselves. As an extra bonus, these artisans are often at the auction, and bidders can meet and chat with the men and women who weave the rugs.

Main St. H-1
Crownpoint, NM 87313
http://www.crownpointrugauction.com/

Important tip: Don't bid on a rug you haven't seen up close. Rugs look quite different on stage.

The biggest city in the Four Corners area, Farmington welcomes visitors with its own unique charms, and makes an excellent hub for local trips.

The name of the area comes from the rare confluence of state boundaries—Utah, Arizona, Colorado, and New Mexico meet in a way that creates four corners. This, of course, has led to photos of people with arms and legs stretched out into each of the four states.

The point of contact is on Navajo Nation land 60 miles northwest of Farmington. The park is known as the **Four Corners Monument** as well as the **Four Corners Tribal Park**. There is a five dollar, cash-only admission charge. The nearest ATM is five miles away at Teec Nos Pos, Arizona, so come prepared. And don't forget your camera because you'll want a souvenir of the day you were in four states simultaneously.
Highway 160 and NM State Highway 597
(928) 206-2540
http://www.navajonationparks.org/htm/fourcorners.htm

The name **B-Square Ranch** is the umbrella for B-Square Ranch's Bolack Museum of Fish and Wildlife, Bolack Electromechanical Museum, and the B-Square Ranch and Experimental Farm. Originally a ranch founded by the late Tommy Bolack, the facility became a private wildlife refuge, a ranch, and farm.

The Bolack Museum of Fish and Wildlife is a private collection of animal specimens (a collection of over 2,500 mounted animals from five continents), while the Bolack Electromechanical Museum displays scientific and technological artifacts.
3901 Bloomfield Highway
Farmington, NM 87401
(505) 325-4275
http://www.bolackmuseum.com

Intrepid explorers and hikers can also explore the area's **Pueblitos (Little Pueblos)** built in the late seventeenth and

early eighteenth centuries and early Navajo rock art.
https://farmingtonnm.org/listings/dinetah-rock-art-pueblitos

The **Bisti Wilderness** is a landscape of strange and striking rock formations of all shapes that is perfect for hikers and photographers. The Wilderness area covers roughly 60 square miles of remote badlands south of Farmington. Once the coastal swamp of an inland sea, the Bisti Wilderness was home to reptiles, dinosaurs, and primitive mammals. Visitors can explore the fossils left behind in the landforms. Note that road conditions can be tricky, and there are no sources of water within the Bisti Wilderness. Bring water with you.
Road 7297, off of Highway 371
South of Farmington, NM
(505) 564-7600
http://www.blm.gov/nm/st/en/prog/blm_special_areas/wilderness_an d_wsas/wilderness_areas/bisti.html

Learn more about restaurants and lodging at
https://farmingtonnm.org/

GALLUP

At the western end of the state, just before the Arizona border on I-40, Gallup is one of the state's original Route 66 towns. It's also in the heart of the Zuni, Hopi, and Navajo Nation lands. Native American arts and crafts are for sale almost everywhere in the city. The city hosts a large rodeo every year that attracts professional cowboys.

Many of the stores are trading companies and take in items as pawn, which can result in some unusual pieces for sale. There is plenty of new jewelry, pottery,

Did You Know...

New Mexico's Official State Necklace Is the Squash Blossom? New Mexico didn't stop with a state gem (the beloved turquoise). It went ahead and designated a piece of jewelry made with those stones as the state necklace. The Squash Blossom necklace was officially adopted by the State Legislature as the state's Official Necklace in 2011.

rugs and unique Native American items available. With over half a dozen trading companies, there's much to explore in a compact, easily walked historic district.

Perhaps the best place to start your exploration of Native American art is at **Richardson's Trading Company**, which has everything from old pawn to contemporary Native American jewelry and other artisan creations (many pieces signed by the artist). The store has many different craft items as well as a room filled with Navajo rugs.
222 W 66th Ave.
Gallup, NM 87301
(505) 722 4762
http://www.richardsontrading.com

There's more than Native American art in Gallup. The town is also a canvas for **wall murals** on publicly and privately owned buildings. Don't miss the **Navajo Code Talkers**, created by artist Be Sargent, on South Second Street between Coal Avenue and Route 66. The Chamber of Commerce also has a small display on the Code Talkers. Find the locations and descriptions of all the murals at http://www.gallupedc.com/gallup/living-here/downtown.

Gallup is also one of the cities along Route 66, and one stellar building from that era still welcomes visitors. During Hollywood's golden years of the 1940s and 1950s, stars often stayed at the El Rancho Hotel while filming Westerns.

The **El Rancho** has been polished up and gleams with movie memorabilia and original design and décor. Visit the gift shop for a good selection of Native American jewelry and pottery. A popular tour stop, it is still open for business for food, lodging, or just a walk through the memorabilia-lined lobby.
1000 E Highway 66
Gallup, NM 87301
(505) 863-9311
http://route66hotels.org/

Gallup also scores in the architecture department with its gem, **El Morro Theatre**, which opened in 1928. The El Morro was designed by Carl Boller, who also designed the KiMo Theater in

Albuquerque and the Lensic Theater in Santa Fe, three stellar buildings.

Visitors may recognize the Pueblo Deco style that was popular in the Southwest. It fused the geometric elements of Art Deco with the themes and artistic touches of Pueblo Revival, as well as a love of murals. Restored in 1991, El Morro is operated by the City of Gallup and is used for movie screenings, performing arts, and other cultural events. Check their website for event information.
207 W Coal Ave.
Gallup, NM 87301
(505) 726-0050
http://www.elmorrotheatre.com/

SPECIAL FOCUS: NAVAJO CODE TALKERS

There are some events that take place during war that cannot be told until decades later. One example of this is the machine that broke the Enigma code. Developed for the British by the team led by the brilliant computer scientist Allan Turing, that computer allowed the Allied forces to intercept and understand coded German information, providing enormous benefits to the war effort.

Another closely kept war secret was the Navajo Code Talkers. Instead of cracking codes, the Navajo Code Talkers created codes. Their language, with a slightly tweaked vocabulary, became a code no one could decipher. During the war years, the Navajo language wasn't yet a written language, and it was almost entirely unknown outside of the Navajo Nation. It's a language with complex tonal qualities and syntax.

In transforming the language into a code, Navajo words were used for war-related machinery. "Hummingbird" was used for fighter planes. "Whale" was used for battleships. In cases where no Navajo word could be used, the word was spelled using Navajo letter sounds.

Code Talkers participated in every major operation in the Pacific theater that involved the Marines. They transmitted tactical information over telephone and radio. Around 400 Navajo were involved in the Code Talker program.

In 2000, President Bill Clinton awarded the Congressional Gold Medal to the original 29 Code Talkers. President George W. Bush presented the medals to the surviving Code Talkers at a ceremony held in the Capitol Rotunda in 2001.

Major Howard Connor, who was the Navajo signal officer at Iwo Jima, said, "Were it not for the Navajos, the Marines would never have taken Iwo Jima."

The story inspired the 2002 movie Windtalkers, starring Nicholas Cage and First Nations actor, Adam Beach.

The last Navajo Code Talker, Chester Nez, died in Albuquerque in 2014 at 93. He was born in Chi Chil Tah, New Mexico, which is southwest of Gallup.

Watch a brief interview with Code Talker, Roy Hawthorne:
https://www.youtube.com/watch?v=ciFv_ONffdw

Learn more about the Code Talkers:
https://www.cia.gov/news-information/featured-story-archive/2008-featured-story-archive/navajo-code-talkers/

Read the story of one of the original Code Talkers:
https://www.cia.gov/news-information/featured-story-archive/2008-featured-story-archive/all-in-the-family.html

Located between Grants and Gallup, **El Morro National Monument** is about an hour south on Highway 53. It's known for its ancient and not-so-ancient inscriptions left by everyone from the Ancestral Puebloans forward. You can walk the paved, half-mile Inscription Loop Trail to see the over two thousand markings from petroglyphs to I was here inscriptions of Spanish soldiers and anyone else going through the area. And come they did—there was a waterhole at the bottom of the sandstone upthrust. Hike to the top of the bluff for views of the ancient ruins.
(505) 783-4226 ext. 801
http://www.nps.gov/elmo/index.htm

GRANTS-MILAN (SEE ALSO ACOMA PUEBLO)

Located on what had been Route 66 (it is now I-40), Grants has attracted its share of tourists over the years. But the biggest economic explosion happened when a Navajo shepherd named Paddy Martinez discovered uranium ore near Haystack Mountain. The mining boom that followed lasted until the 1980s and gave Grants the nickname of the "Uranium Capital of the World."

The real star of the town is underground. Visitors to the **New Mexico Mining Museum** enter an elevator and go down one floor into the subterranean world of a mine. Your mind may tell you that you're not underground, but all around you are warning signs, carts, rails, tools, and the detritus of mining operations. Audio stations along the way have actual miners talking about the different aspects of the mining process. In fact, the consultants on the project were former miners. The focus is on uranium, but the process is similar for any type of ore that has to be wrested from the ground.

Before heading below, sit in one of the comfortable chairs and watch the video on mining. It provides background that will be useful when you push the red buttons that activate the narrative along the tour.

Though thorough and comprehensive, there is one huge topic the museum doesn't address—uranium disasters. Thus, the Mining Museum becomes a fascinating, but one-sided show on nuclear power. The handout on the discovery and production of uranium further supports the unspoken idea that it's all about technology. All gain, and no risk.

That attitude probably explains why there is not a word about the Church Rock disaster, the uranium mill spill that occurred in New Mexico in 1979 when United Nuclear Corporation's Church Rock uranium mill tailings disposal pond breached its dam.
100 N Iron Ave.
Grants, New Mexico
(800) 748-2142

Strangely enough, there is also significant air travel history in Grants. What do you use to guide airplanes if you don't have sophisticated tracking systems or even radio? The answer turns out to be huge concrete arrows and a system of land-based lighthouses. In the early 1920s, the federal government built this system across the United States to keep planes flying safely along pre-established air routes. New Mexico was part of the route between Amarillo and Los Angeles, and some of this history remains open to visitors.

Most of the lighthouses have been torn down for salvage or have fallen into disrepair. Only a few of the beacons and their tiny houses remain. The remnants of these concrete arrows are indistinguishable from random chunks of cement. However, eager seekers can find some using online information:
http://www.dreamsmithphotos.com/arrow/arrows.html

Beyond the arrows, you can find more substantial remains of this part of aviation history in the **Grants-Milan Airport and Aviation Heritage Museum**, which is actually one of the tiny houses—140-square-foot Beacon Hut #62. It's finding new life with special exhibits, including old pictures, plane parts, and other memorabilia. Next to the hut is the old beacon. After years of restoration, the site has been listed on the National Register of Historic Places (2015).

There's another beacon that is open to visitors. **Beacon Hut #61** sits atop a ridge on the Continental Divide at the Oso Ridge Fire Lookout. The site includes the base of the long-gone beacon tower and the original generator hut that housed the power to light the airway beacon. There's also a 1930s cabin that once served as the residence. According to Cibola County Historical Society, the site is now a satellite location for the Grants facility. Visitors should call ahead to arrange a visit. (505) 287-4700
http://www.cibolahistory.org/aviation-heritage-museum.html

The stunning **El Malpais National Monument** is about 30 miles from Grants. Malpais means badlands in Spanish, but beautiful might be a better way to describe the landscape. Yes, it is a bleak beauty, but it is also total silence surrounded by

mesas and volcanic fields with a dormant volcano in the distant background. The 350,000 acres include scenic drives, self-guided trails, caves, and lava tubes. Don't miss La Ventana Natural Arch, the largest of its kind in New Mexico. There are several ways into the monument, and different areas offer different sights and attractions.
http://www.nps.gov/elma/index.htm

Learn more about attractions in Grants-Milan at:
http://www.grants.org/museums-galleries.aspx

SHIPROCK

Part of Navajo Nation land (and also considered part of the Farmington Metropolitan area), Shiprock gets its name from the 1,600-foot-tall uplift—actually an eroded volcanic plume—that oversees the plains around it. The site is considered sacred to the Navajo. Its English name comes from the formation's resemblance to a nineteenth-century clipper ship.

There is no direct road, but drivers often spot it going south out of the town of Shiprock, looking west near Highway 491. Visitors have been known to take dirt roads to get a bit closer.

NORTH CENTRAL

Some of the most dramatic mountain and forest scenery in New Mexico can be found in the North Central part of the state. Much of that beauty is incorporated into the scenic Enchanted Circle, a ring of towns that offer spectacular views and outdoor adventure. This area also includes the magnet towns of Taos and Santa Fe.

A loop of roads that circles back to Taos, the Enchanted Circle includes several small towns and staggering views. Snowcapped Wheeler Peak rises 13,161 feet above sea level and has the distinction of being the tallest mountain in New Mexico.

The Enchanted Circle route is NM 522 between Taos and Questa; NM 38 between Questa, the Red River Valley, and Eagle Nest; and NM 434 between Eagle Nest and Angel Fire. It sounds more complicated than it is. On a map and on the road, it's quite easy to follow.

Take NM 64 east for a gorgeous detour to historic Cimarron, then back south via I-25, or loop back to Taos on NM 64 through the Carson National Forest.

The North Central region is also the destination for visitors who want to enjoy the arts of Santa Fe and Taos. Visitors have their choice of two routes linking these cities. The scenic byway called the High Road (SR 76) highlights several towns and is considered more scenic, offering striking vistas. The Low Road (SR 68) is a bit faster and shadows the Rio Grande River, taking drivers past small towns and farms and giving peeks of the river. The usual compromise is to take one road up and the other road back for a complete scenic experience.

If you're using a GPS, the easiest way to get to the High Road is to set your GPS for Chimayo. For the Low Road, set it for Embudo Station or Dixon.

The other scenic byway is the Turquoise Trail (Route 14) between Albuquerque and Santa Fe. The best views can be found when driving north. A compromise here is to take Route 14 one way for the views and use I-25 to go back for the speed and convenience.

ABIQUIÚ

Abiquiú is best known for its association with Georgia O'Keeffe. The town itself has a church, a diminutive public library, and a few houses set around a dusty center. There's a general store by the town's gas station and a restaurant. Although not a tree-shaded oasis, Abiquiú Lake is large enough for boating and has a picnic area and campground. http://www.recreation.gov/camping/riana--abiquiu-lake/r/campgroundDetails.do?contractCode=NRSO&parkId=73364

The draw here is the spectacular beauty of **Ghost Ranch**, spread over 21,000 acres. It is heavily linked in most people's minds with the art of Georgia O'Keeffe, who not only painted here but also owned a small piece of land here as well.

The intriguing name is said to have come from the cattle rustlers who used to hide their stolen goods in the area and wanted to discourage neighbors from nosing around. The original name Rancho de los Brujos (Ranch of the Witches) eventually became Ghost Ranch.

Today Ghost Ranch is owned by the Presbyterian Church, who open it to the public for tours (including the popular O'Keeffe Trail Ride and Tour), workshops, hiking, and more. The setting is gorgeous—the rock formations and colors are clearly the inspiration for O'Keeffe's art.
1708 Highway 84
Abiquiú, NM
(505) 685-4333
Toll Free: (877) 804-4678
http://ghostranch.org/

O'Keeffe didn't live at Ghost Ranch full time. Her main residence is up a steep, paved road in Abiquiú. Tours of the **Georgia O'Keeffe House** are available only through the O'Keeffe Museum, and you must make arrangements in advance. You won't be able to bring a camera or even a notebook, but your eye and mind can record. The gardens are lovely. The junipers, sage, lawn, and house look much as she left them.
(505) 685-4539
http://www.okeeffemuseum.org/abiquiu-home--studio.html

In this delightful clip O'Keeffe talks about how she started her series on bones she found at her home in New Mexico. Fans will definitely enjoy this.
https://www.youtube.com/watch?v=v71awD38Qy4

SPECIAL FOCUS: GEORGIA O'KEEFFE

Although born in Wisconsin, Georgia O'Keeffe (1887-1986) is a beloved New Mexican artist who created some of the most iconic images of the landscape she loved. The Georgia O'Keeffe Museum in Santa Fe considers her one of the most significant and intriguing artists of the twentieth century.

O'Keeffe was trained as a realist but found a more abstract orientation better suited her artistic vision. She often cropped her paintings—much like photographers did—to create intense close-ups. O'Keeffe painted in series, focusing on a theme and exploring it throughout several paintings. Her lushly painted flowers remain a vibrant example of her groundbreaking perspective.

The inexorable trajectory of her fame began in 1915 when O'Keeffe sent some of her early designs to a friend in New York City who showed them to Alfred Stieglitz. Stieglitz (1864–1946) was a famous art dealer and internationally known photographer. He arranged for an exhibition of her work in his gallery. He and O'Keeffe later married.

Stieglitz is considered a major American photographer who made significant contributions to photographic art. He realized the potential of the photographic image to take reality and render it with a fresh eye. He created abstractions from the everyday world and turned his artistic eye to the urban landscape, documenting its changes. He took small moments and rendered them large enough for us to see and appreciate.

In 1929, at the invitation of Dorothy Brett and Mabel Dodge Luhan, Georgia O'Keeffe came to visit New Mexico and fell in love with the landscape. While there, O'Keeffe discovered Ghost Ranch, a discovery which ultimately changed the direction of her paintings. She made her home there, and the starkly colorful beauty of the landscape became one of her most famous themes.

Visitors to Ghost Ranch who are familiar with her paintings are often struck by the realization that her dramatic, perhaps even surreal, landscapes were actual depictions of what she saw around her. It's even possible to recognize some of the unique features in her paintings. Pedernal, the flat-topped mountain, was one of her favorites. She is famously quoted, "God told me if I painted that mountain enough, I could have it" (Laurie Lisle in Portrait of an Artist, 1980).

She eventually convinced Arthur Park, who was the owner the Ranch, to sell her a small piece of land that would become her summer home. Later, she bought land and a crumbling house in Abiquiú, which she renovated for year-round living.

For the next two decades O'Keeffe lived and painted in New Mexico. Despite her deep love of the land, it wasn't until 1949, several years after Stieglitz died, that she formally moved to Abiquiú.

Toward the end of her life, O'Keeffe moved to Santa Fe, where she died after nearly a century of being an American and New Mexican iconic figure.

ANGEL FIRE

This ski and resort town is a significant Enchanted Circle tourist destination and a perfect base for exploring the area.

People come in winter for its downhill skiing, snowmobiling, and cross-country skiing. In summer, the cooler temperatures of the high mountains welcome visitors for fishing, golf, mountain biking, and ATV fun.

Note: Winter is the real tourist season here. Some of the restaurants will not be open in summer.

Large, sprawling resorts are few in New Mexico. Enchanted Circle lodging is mainly found in Taos and at the intimate inns and tiny hotels scattered throughout the area. But there is one exception. **Angel Fire Resort** draws visitors year round. It offers mountain biking, hiking, and zip-lining in the summer, but it really comes alive in winter with downhill skiing and other snow-based activities.
10 Miller Lane
Angel Fire, NM 87710
(575) 377-6401
http://www.angelfireresort.com/

The town has a more serious side. Angel Fire is also home to the **Vietnam Veterans Memorial**. Built in 1968 by Dr. and Mrs. Westphall to honor the memory of their son, 1st LT David Westphall, and 53 others who were killed in action in Vietnam on May 22, 1968, it was the first major Vietnam memorial in the country. The memorial incorporates a dramatic design with a chapel that soars to 50 feet, designed by Santa Fe architect Ted Luna. Today it is called Vietnam Veterans Memorial State Park.
34 Country Road
Angel Fire, NM 87710
(575) 377-6900
https://www.vietnamveteransmemorial.org/

CERRILLOS

Cerrillos lies on the Turquoise Trail (Route 14) linking Santa Fe and Albuquerque, but unlike Madrid, which is just down the road, Cerrillos is slowly descending into ghost town status. The only real bright spot is the Visitor Center for the Cerrillos Hills State Park.

Turquoise and the railroad made this town famous. The early Native Americans mined the stone, and the Spanish came to do so as well. It is said that the turquoise from Cerrillos found its way to the crown jewels of Spain. Miners came to the area to prospect for gold, silver, lead, zinc, and turquoise—peaking in the 1880s. At one time, the town had over a dozen saloons and several hotels as a result of the hundreds of mines throughout the hills.

The train still roars through but no longer stops; the turquoise mines are almost played out. Some of the old buildings still stand, but most are either vacant or for sale. Plaques on several of these buildings tell visitors their story.

Currently there is still a bar, Mary's, and **St. Joseph's Church** from 1922, which was built to replace the original church from 1884. The town has a fascinating website with more information on its history.
http://www.cerrillosnewmexico.com/cerrillos-historical-society

The **Casa Grande Trading Post** is relatively new, built in 1975 by Todd and Patricia Brown. It sells turquoise and jewelry from their own turquoise mine as well as mining artifacts and antiques.
17 Waldo St.
Cerrillos, NM 87010
(505) 438-3008
http://www.casagrandetradingpost.com/

Cerrillos State Park offers guided walks at the park entrance a half mile from town on CR 59. There's a five dollar fee to enter the park. Walks usually take place at 2:00 p.m. on Saturday, but you can hike the trails any time the park is open, including the trails that go past some of the old mines. Other programs, including talks and special events, take place at the Visitor Center.
37 Main St.
Cerrillos, NM 87010
(505) 474-0196
http://www.emnrd.state.nm.us/SPD/cerrilloshillsstatepark.html

CHAMA

Chama is the main starting point for the famous **Cumbres & Toltec Scenic Railroad**, a three-foot, narrow-gauge heritage railroad that began in 1880 to serve the San Juan Colorado

mining district. When the country switched to the wider gauge lines and the silver boom waned, the line was never upgraded. Today the line runs between Chama, New Mexico and Antonito, Colorado, but the train only goes one way. Passengers take a motor coach ride back to their starting point. The station is in the center of Chama along NM Highway 17.
500 Terrace Ave.
Chama, NM 87520
(888) 286-2737
http://cumbrestoltec.com/

CHIMAYO

One of the highlights of the High Road to Taos, Chimayo is known for its church and its weavers. It has a rich and fascinating history, reflected in its present-day lagniappe. The town has developed and sells its own Chimayo red chile.

The **Santuario de Chimayo** is a stunning and often-photographed wood and adobe church that opened in 1816. It still offers daily mass for the community and its visitors.

Chimayo is said to be the site of a miracle that occurred 200 years ago. This chapel, now commonly called el Santuario de Chimayo, is the destination of thousands of pilgrims.

Stop in the welcome center for information or wander the area. Additional highlights include the Three Cultures Monument and the sculpture of St. Francis, but there are religious monuments throughout the Sanctuary area. Take CR 98 and follow the signs to Santuario de Chimayo.
15 Santuario Drive
Chimayo, NM 87522
(505) 351-9961
http://www.elsantuariodechimayo.us/

Chimayo is also justifiably famous for its weavers. The early Hispanic settlers brought a particular type of Churro sheep that thrived in the New Mexico climate. The fleece of the sheep became an important part of the economic life of the area, and Chimayo families became known for weavings that were prized up and down the trade routes. Today, the Ortegas and the Trujillos form dynasties and have trained hundreds of weavers to grow this beautiful artistic niche.

Ortega's is located at the entrance to the road leading to the church at CR 98 and SR 76, selling their rugs, blankets, coats, and bags, as well as jewelry and pottery.
CR 98 at NM 76
Chimayo, NM 87522
(505) 351-4215
http://www.OrtegasWeaving.com

Trujillo's weaving shop is another good stop. It's located at the far end of town shortly before the turnoff for CR 98. There is usually someone weaving on one of the looms.
814 NM-76
Chimayo, NM 87522
(505) 351-4457

Centinela Traditional Arts is the tapestry gallery of Irvin and Lisa Trujillo. They represent other fiber artists as well.
946 State Road 76
Chimayo, NM 87522
(505) 351-2180
http://www.chimayoweavers.com

While in Chimayo, pick up some of the **local Chimayo red chile**. It's sold almost everywhere in town.

The appellation is a United States Patent and Trademark Office (USPTO) registered certification mark owned by Chimayo Chile Farmers, Inc., which works to keep the chile strain pure and a product of Chimayo.

Is it genuine? If the package says "New Mexican" chile rather than Chimayo chile (Capsicum annum "Chimayo"), it isn't truly Chimayo chile. The Chimayo chile has a different flavor profile that has more flavor than heat (although remember that what a New Mexican considers mild, other parts of the country may consider hotter). It is well worth tracking down.
http://www.nativehispanic.com/

DIXON

Dixon is one of the Low Road towns located just off SR 68 on SR 75. The presence of water from the Embudo River, a tributary of the Rio Grande, has made this a farming area. There are artists and galleries and a historic church. The town also has two wineries that welcome tasters.

Vivac Winery is just off SR 75.
2075 NM-68
Dixon, NM 87527
(505) 579-4441
http://vivacwinery.com/

La Chiripada Winery is located in the town itself.
NM-75
Dixon, NM 87527
(505 579-4437
http://lachiripada.com/

Dixon has been home to the autumn Dixon Studio Tour since 1982. Many of the artists are in Dixon, but the tour also encompasses those in Rinconada and other nearby towns. http://www.dixonarts.org/

The beautiful **Embudo Mission** was once a mission school opened in 1911. The community has restored it to a small meeting space with accommodations.
(505) 579-4111
http://www.missionembudo.com/

Across NM 75 from Embudo Mission, **St. Anthony de Padua** dates back to 1929 and still offers services.
1114 Private Drive
Dixon, NM 87527

For many years, Dixon was the destination of apple lovers who headed to the famous **Dixon's Apple Orchard**. Sadly, the orchards were destroyed by wildfire and floods in 2011, and owners Jim and Becky Mullane moved to Wisconsin. Even though it is still sometimes mentioned as an attraction unfortunately this famous family-friendly spot no longer exists.

DULCE

In reality, Dulce is the tribal headquarters of the Jicarilla Apache Reservation. But in matters of speculation, it's a hotbed of alien life. Dulce Base is an alleged secret alien underground facility under Archuleta Mesa. It makes for fun, but totally unproven speculation. http://en.wikipedia.org/wiki/Dulce_Base

EDGEWOOD

Located along I-40 and part of the state's Route 66 history, Edgewood began as a farming town settled by families seeking to take advantage of the Homestead Act that bestowed land in exchange for homesteading. Today, Edgewood is close enough to Albuquerque to be a commuter community.

The lure for visitors is **Wildlife West Nature Park**, an environmental education center, licensed zoological park, and wildlife refuge. They also offer some fun public events, including their chuck wagon dinners and music festivals.
Edgewood, NM 87015
(877) 981-9453
http://www.wildlifewest.org/

EMBUDO

A Low Road (SR 68) town between Santa Fe and Taos, Embudo is a ghost town, but of the recent variety. Up until a few years ago, Embudo Station was a restaurant along the Rio Grande, reached by a concrete bridge that still provides a lovely view of the river.

However, Embudo still requires a visit because the area is home to **Johnnie Meier Classical Gas Museum** on Gasoline Alley. Visitors are amazed at the incredible collection of car- and gasoline-related memorabilia. You will see old cars, defunct gasoline pumps, a sweet-looking blue and white diner complete with cheery tables in front, and much more.
1819 Highway 68
Embudo, NM 87531
(505) 852-2995

ESPANOLA (SEE ALSO SANTA CLARA PUEBLO)

Located between Albuquerque and Santa Fe, the town itself offers a wildlife center and easy access to Puye Cliffs of the Santa Clara Pueblo.

The **Wildlife Center** just north of Santa Fe rehabilitates injured and orphaned animals with the aim of returning them to the wild. Self-guided tours take visitors alongside the enclosures of raptors, bobcats, gray foxes, and more. There are also docent-led tours.

43

19 Wheat St.
Espanola, New Mexico 87532
(505) 753-9505
http://thewildlifecenter.org

FORT BURGWIN

At mile marker 65.8 on Highway 518 (just south of Taos), today Fort Burgwin is an office of **Southern Methodist University** in Taos, but it was built as a temporary fort in 1852 to protect the wagons traveling the road from Santa Fe to Taos. It also served as headquarters for regional military operations. Since it was never meant to be permanent, it was abandoned when it was no longer needed.

In the 1950s, a lumber company owned the property. The company's owner, Ralph Rounds, was an amateur archaeologist. Eventually, Rounds, with the help of SMU archaeologist Fred Wendorf, found the remnants of the log fort, excavated it, and rebuilt it to look like the original structure. It is now the summer campus of SMU-in-Taos, and the fort is the main office. The school offers special events that are free and open to the public.
https://www.smu.edu/Taos/Events

GOLDEN

This almost gone town is home to **Henderson General Store** which offers everything from general merchandise to jewelry, pottery, and rugs.
1710 State Highway 14 N
Golden, NM 87047
(505) 281-7136
http://www.hendersonstore.com/index.html

HERNANDEZ

Hernandez is best known as the subject of a 1941 Ansel Adams photograph, **Moonrise, Hernandez, New Mexico**. It is generally agreed that the photo was taken late in the afternoon on November 1, 1941 from a shoulder of US Route 84. The town is five miles northwest of Espanola on US Routes 84/285.

It's not possible to reproduce the photo, but you can learn more about its origin at https://en.wikipedia.org/wiki/Moonrise,_Hernandez,_New_Mexico

LAMY

Lamy derived its name from Jean Baptiste Lamy, the first Archbishop of Santa Fe, who was the inspiration for Willa Cather's famous novel, Death Comes for the Archbishop.

Like so many other towns in New Mexico, Lamy was a town on 1the Atchison, Topeka & Santa Fe Railroad (AS&SF). The line was originally planned to run from Atchison, Kansas, on the Missouri River, to Santa Fe, the capital city of New Mexico. However, engineers decided that the hills surrounding Santa Fe made this impractical. They decided instead to build the railway line though Lamy, which was eighteen miles away. From Lamy, they'd create a spur line to Santa Fe.

As the nearest stop to Santa Fe, the town had a role in the development of the atomic bomb. Since Los Alamos was top secret, no one was supposed to live there. Everyone who came to New Mexico to work on the Manhattan Project got off the train at Lamy and then went up to Santa Fe before heading to Los Alamos.

In fact, if you're traveling on the Southwest Chief trains Three and Four to Santa Fe, you still have to get off at Lamy and take a shuttle bus to Santa Fe. If you are leaving from Santa Fe on that train, you reverse the process and shuttle over to Lamy.

The Burlington Northern Santa Fe (BNSF) still passes through Lamy, but few people leave the train to explore the town.

In New Mexico history, the railroad was one of the creators (and destroyers) of towns. When the railroad came to Lamy, the town thrived. In 1896, the Fred Harvey Company built the grand El Ortiz Hotel here. Fred Harvey was quite a force for New Mexico's early tourism. His company owned the Harvey House chain of restaurants, hotels, and hospitality businesses that enabled visitors to comfortably travel and tour the Southwest. As with too many of these grand old hotels, the El Ortiz is no more.

There is a **Lamy Railroad & History Museum**, which is open by appointment only. It's in the Legal, originally built in 1881 as the Browne and Manzanares General Store.
151 Old Lamy Trail
Lamy, NM 87540
(505) 466-1650
http://www.lamymuseum.org/

SPECIAL FOCUS: FRED HARVEY AND HIS MAGNIFICENT HOTELS

Perhaps the best way to sum up the impact of Fred Harvey is the line written by Frank Waters in his 1950 book Masked Gods: "the Fred Harvey system introduced America to Americans."

Harvey had a true pull-yourself-up-by-your-bootstraps life, but the interesting part, especially for New Mexico, began when he realized that trains offered abysmal food to their trapped passengers.

Living in Kansas at the time, Harvey approached the Kansas Pacific railway with a plan to open decent eateries by the train stations. He was promptly turned down. Not a man easily dissuaded, Harvey went to the Atchison, Topeka, and Santa Fe Railway (AT&SF), and that was the beginning of the golden age of train tourism in New Mexico.

Harvey revolutionized the hospitality industry by creating a series of restaurants, hotels, and gift shops at all the major stops of the AT&SF railway. At the time, the AT&SF was not only the major rail system in the Southwest, it was a purveyor of travel experiences that were simply unavailable anywhere else in the world. Although he eventually operated in 80 cities across the country, it was in New Mexico that Harvey made his greatest impact.

Instead of speeding through New Mexico, the railway decided to make Wild West travel a lure. It opened opulent landmark hotels across the state. Travel through New Mexico would never be as sumptuous again.

The company began advertising their Southwestern Indian Detours. By the late nineteenth century, Americans who could afford it were traveling to the Southwest, staying in luxury hotels, learning about Indian arts and crafts (and buying those artisan products in gift shops), and going deep into Indian Country on special tours.

Harvey left a legacy of stunning hotels with fresh food and grand lodging. Architect and designer Mary Colter worked with Harvey to create lush Southwest-inspired interiors.

But it was not to last. The automobile came along, and the railroad, the towns, and the hotels faded. In one of the saddest times in the history of architecture, Harvey hotels languished and were destroyed.

Some of the finest examples of Mission-style design were demolished—the Alvarado in Albuquerque, El Navajo in Gallup, El Ortiz in Lamy, and many more. But the bright spots in the state are La Fonda in Santa Fe, which is still welcoming guests, and the Castaneda in Las Vegas, which is undergoing extensive renovations in preparation for reopening under developer Allan Affeldt.

The New Mexico History Museum in Santa Fe is offering a long-term special exhibit on Fred Harvey. Setting the Standard: The Fred Harvey Company and Its Legacy is showing now through December 31, 2030.

Learn more at: http://newmexicohistory.org/people/fred-harvey-civilizer-of-the-west

Mary Colter: https://en.wikipedia.org/wiki/Mary_Colter

LAS TRAMPAS

The High Road town of Las Trampas, which is 30 miles south of Taos, is notable for its church, **San Jose de Garcia**, built around the 1760s.

The church is said to be open on Fridays and Saturdays, but the hours are irregular. Although it's part of a recognized historic district, little else seems to be intact. But if you're on the High Road, the architecture of the church is worth a visit.

LOS ALAMOS

Most visitors are surprised to learn that Los Alamos (The Cottonwoods) had a history before the United States Government turned it into a top-secret Manhattan Project base. A Detroit businessman named Ashley Pond started Los Alamos Ranch School in 1917 as a boy's school where "privileged Eastern boys might become robust, learned men."

In 1943, the school closed and the scientists moved in. Ironically, the buildings that can be visited date back to the school, not the town's atomic history. However, that will change. The National Park Service is in the process of setting up a new **Manhattan Project National Historical Park** that will encompass major atomic sites in Hanford, NH, Oakridge, TN, and, of course, our own Los Alamos.

Opening date has not yet been determined, but the Los Alamos buildings scheduled to be included are: Gun Site and V-Site facilities as well as TA-18-1 Slotin Building, TA-18-2 Battleship Control Building, and TA-18-29 Pond Cabin. This will open the town to even more visitors who are interested in exploring its unique atomic bomb history. Learn more here: http://www.atomicheritage.org/article/manhattan-project-national-historical-park-memorandum-agreement-released

Fuller Lodge, constructed using 771 pine logs, started as a dining room for the school and metamorphosed into lodging during the Manhattan Project years. Designed by famous New Mexico architect, John Gaw Meem, the building is now a cultural center.

Located in a wing of the Lodge, Fuller Lodge Art Center offers one-day and short-term art classes for adults and children, plus rotating exhibits of professional and emerging artists centered on some intriguing themes. Their Gallery Shop features the work of over ninety local and regional artists.

2132 Central Ave.
Los Alamos, NM 87544
(505) 662-1635
http://fullerlodgeartcenter.com/

Other buildings from the school were repurposed for the war effort. The **Los Alamos Historical Society** offers docent-led tours. Their website has a downloadable walking tour map. They are headquartered in a building located on Bathtub Row, named after the amenity included in the housing constructed for the school's faculty that was not available to the later-arriving scientists.
1050 Bathtub Row
Los Alamos, NM 87544
(505) 662-6272
http://www.losalamoshistory.org/

The **Bradbury Science Museum** is definitely worth a stop, especially if you're traveling with children. It's named after Norris Bradbury, who was the Director of LANL (not the famous science fiction author). Forty interactive exhibits focus on the Manhattan Project history as well as the Lab's current research projects. The Bradbury Museum is also free.
1350 Central Ave.
Los Alamos, NM 87544
(505) 667-4444
http://www.lanl.gov/museum/

Mesa Public Library was designed by famed New Mexico architect, Antoine Predock. The building is known for its angles and curves as well as the views of the Jemez Mountains. The gallery features local artists and exhibits and special programs.
2400 Central Ave.
Los Alamos, NM 87544
(505) 662-8242
https://www.losalamosnm.us/library/Pages/MPL.aspx

Los Alamos has another surprising aspect. It has the only NHL-regulation-sized outdoor **refrigerated ice rink** in New Mexico (open in winter).
4475 West Road
Los Alamos, NM 87544
(505) 662-4500
https://www.losalamosnm.us/rec/rink/Pages/default.aspx

In addition to history, the city is home to **Don Quixote Distillery**, established in 2005 as New Mexico's first fully licensed and bonded distillery. It specializes in New Mexico agricultural products. Distillers Ron and Olha Dolhin take their craft seriously, perfecting not only their spirits but their stills.
236 Rio Bravo
Los Alamos, NM 87544
(505) 695-0817
http://dqdistillery.com/about.html

Los Alamos makes a good base for exploring the area. There are several lodging options and there are plenty of restaurants. Important sites of history and beauty are nearby. The Jemez Mountain Trail National Scenic Byway between Los Alamos and San Ysidro takes drivers to several important monuments, including Jemez State Monument, Bandelier National Monument, and the one million-year-old Valles Caldera.
http://www.jemezmountaintrail.org/

SPECIAL FOCUS: CHOOSING LOS ALAMOS FOR THE A-BOMB

The most crucial part of the development of the A-Bomb was its creation. It had to be done someplace no one could find; someplace almost no one even knew existed.

J. Robert Oppenheimer was the brilliant administrator of the bomb design project, and he selected Los Alamos largely because of a near-fatal bout with dysentery.

New Mexico had developed a reputation in the 1920s as a haven for people with health problems. The pure air, abundant sunshine, and generally good weather was thought to be healing. In 1922, Oppenheimer was an 18-year-old who needed to recover from a very serious case of dysentery. His family sent him, along with one of his teachers, Herbert Smith, to the Los Alamos Ranch School, located about 25 miles northwest of Santa Fe. Oppenheimer ultimately recovered his health. While there, he developed a deep love of the land that led him to choose Los Alamos for the secret installation.

In addition to its remote location, the area even had buildings that could be used in the nascent facility. In 1918, just a few years before Oppenheimer's arrival, a school had been created, complete with houses, dormitories, and living quarters in addition to some school buildings, an arts and crafts building, a carpentry shop, a small sawmill, barns, garages, sheds, and an ice house.

Not everyone subscribes to this bit of history. In fact, the Los Alamos Historical Society says that Oppenheimer knew of Los Alamos because he had a ranch in the Sangre de Cristo Mountains and had spent time horseback riding in the Jemez. http://www.losalamoshistory.org/manhattan_project.htm

The question remains, how and why did Oppenheimer come to have a ranch in New Mexico? The most sensible answer is that he did come to New Mexico to take the cure (which most agree) and once here, he fell in love with the beauty of New Mexico.

What is certain is that the area of Los Alamos played a crucial part in the development of the bomb and in the country's success in World War II.

MADRID

There are several different levels of ghost town in New Mexico. There are the true ghost towns, where few people live and the buildings are in serious disrepair. There are also semi-ghost towns, where people still live, perhaps with a business or two open, but the economic life of the town is very precarious. Then, there are the towns like Madrid, 2which are a third kind of ghost town: the kind that quite literally came back to life. From thriving coal company town to ghost town, and now a rising phoenix of arts and crafts, Madrid was also the movie set for Wild Hogs. The 2007 film was not only set in Madrid, but identified the town with the correct pronunciation (MAdrid).

The town's buildings line both sides of one of the most scenic routes in the state, the Turquoise Trail, which joins Albuquerque and Santa Fe. It has become a thriving arts community, as a stroll down Route 14 any day of the week makes clear. But there's quirkiness lurking as well.

The **Mineshaft Tavern** has been serving miners, locals, and now visitors in that building since 1946. It's filled with history and has the longest standing bar in the country—about six inches higher than a regular bar and just the right height for standing and drinking.

Just next door is the **Coal Mine Museum**, an eclectic and quirky mix of whatever was deemed worthy to save when the coal mine shut down and the miners left. You'll find everything from an old Model T to one of the earliest X-ray machines in New Mexico.
2846 NM-14
Madrid, NM 87010
(505) 473-0743
http://www.themineshafttavern.com/

SPECIAL FOCUS: MADRID AND WILD HOGS

Although already well known as a Turquoise Trail town, Madrid became famous outside the state with the motorcycle movie, Wild Hogs. Ostensibly shot in Cincinnati, the movie was actually filmed in Albuquerque and Madrid, along with other parts of New Mexico.

After the movie was released, everyone wanted to see the famous Madrid town, especially Maggie's Diner. Although the exterior was created for the movie, today it's a lure for real bikers and other fans of the film who like to have their picture taken in front.

Wild Hogs also showcased the fictional Chile Festival. There was no such festival, but in classic life follows art, the town actually created a chile festival, figuring they may as well take advantage of the buzz created by the movie. The hotel in which the Wild Hogs stayed is actually the town's grocery store, where you can find just about anything you need.

OHKAY OWINGEH (FORMERLY SAN JUAN PUEBLO)

When the Spanish arrived in what was often called the New World, one of the first things they did was to rename the native peoples they found. They renamed Ohkay Owingeh the

San Juan Pueblo, but the Pueblo has since returned to its original name.

The pueblo offers two programs so that visitors can get to know the people of the pueblo and their lives. The leader of the Pueblo Revolt (See Special Focus: Pueblo Revolt of 1680) was from the pueblo located near Santa Fe. Their **Popay tour** is named in his honor.
http://ohkayowingehhousingauthority.org/visitus.php

OJO CALIENTE

Ojo Caliente Mineral Springs Resort & Spa is quite possibly the best hot springs in New Mexico. It is one of the oldest mineral spas in the country, dating back to 1868. But what really sets Ojo Caliente apart is that it is the only hot springs in the world with four different types of mineral water. Lithia, iron, soda, and arsenic all bubble up from the underground springs and are channeled into different pools. Visitors can take their pick of the water in which to soak.

Of course, the history of the springs goes back much further. The land belonged to the Tewa tribe, who built their large pueblos and terraced gardens on the mesa overlooking the springs. The Posi (or Poseouinge) village was the largest in the area and was home to thousands of people. Its ruins are still atop the mesa and are a popular hiking destination.

Ojo Caliente looks a lot different today than when it opened, but some of the original buildings remain and are listed on the National Registry of Historic Places. The Historic Bathhouse, built in 1868, is still used as a bathhouse (although totally renovated and updated inside). The Historic Hotel, built in 1916, has also been updated and offers comfortable rooms, the Artesian Restaurant, and the Wine Bar.

The Adobe Round Barn, built in 1924, is now a special events venue. There's also a bucolic hiking trail around the river that should not be missed. Gentle and lovely.

50 Los Banos Drive
Ojo Caliente, NM 87549
(505) 583-2233
http://www.ojospa.com/

POJOAQUE PUEBLO

As with many of the pueblos of New Mexico, Pojoaque offers
casino gaming, but the people of the pueblo are eager to share
their culture and history through the **Poeh Cultural Center**.
Well worth a visit for the Pueblo art and exhibits, the center
also hosts traditional Indian dances on weekends and
preserves the traditional arts of the Tewa-speaking Pueblos.
78 Cities of Gold Road
Santa Fe, NM 87506
(505) 455-3334
http://www.poehcenter.com

POT CREEK (SEE FORT BURGWIN)

This long-gone ancient pueblo is located along the High Road
between Santa Fe and Taos on the grounds of SMU. It is
unclear what happened to this pueblo. Archeologists at SMU-
in-Taos at Fort Burgwin excavated the thirteenth-century
pueblo and found evidence of structural fires, caused
intentionally. Archeologists investigated the site, but after
excavation, the pueblo was covered back up. There is little left
of the main settlement to see.

However, just down the road at mile marker 66.4 is the **Pot
Creek Cultural Site** in the Carson National Forest. The mile-
long trail includes the remains of several of the buildings as
well as one restored building.

The site is not officially open. Those who wish to visit can pull
off the road, duck under the barrier (easily done) and wander
through what had once been quite a lovely site with trails and
picnic tables. Don't think you're trespassing. The SMU website
itself says, "Visitation is encouraged."
Highway 518 and Mile Marker 66.4
Pot Creek, NM 87571
(575) 587-2255
http://www.smu.edu/Taos/PotCreek

One of the most frequently photographed churches in New Mexico is just south of Taos in Ranchos de Taos. **San Francisco de Asis Mission Church** (also spelled San Francisco de Assisi Mission Church) was completed in 1816. Its architecture is similar to many of the churches in New Mexico—Spanish Colonial with Native American touches. There are two towers that flank the church entrance, each with its own cross, with another cross atop the entrance arch. The two monumental buttress towers make the church feel massive and have drawn artists and photographers. Georgia O'Keeffe painted it in 1929, and Ansel Adams photographed it from the back that same year.

A historic marker in the Rancho de Taos plaza helps visitors find the church, which is located in the back of the parking lot. The main entrance is actually off a side street.

60 St Francis Plaza
Ranchos De Taos, NM 87557
(575) 758-2754
http://www.nps.gov/nr/travel/american_latino_heritage/san_francisc o_de_assisi_mission_church.html

RED RIVER

This Enchanted Circle town is a small charmer. Strung along Route 38, it has a minuscule population (477 as of 2010) and a one-mile long Main Street that gives it a true old-time feel.

Like so many of the towns in New Mexico, its ancestry is that of a mining town. First known as River City, it was the site of gold, silver, and copper mines that were carved into the Sangre de Cristo (Blood of Christ) Mountains. And, as a successful mining town, it was quite lively with saloons, dance halls, and even a red light district. As with many New Mexico towns, when the ore disappeared, so did the people. Sports enthusiasts now visit for the outdoor activities—the traditional winter sports when the snow comes, and hiking, off-roading, and mountain biking when the snow is gone. As an added benefit, the ski runs practically start in town as Red River nestles right up to the mountains. Learn more about Red River at http://www.redriver.org/

The **Little Red School House Museum** was built in 1915 and was used as a schoolhouse until 1942. Hours and access depend on volunteers. It's located on Jayhawk Trail behind the Red River Public Library.
(575) 754-3030
http://redriver.org/schoolhouse

SANTA CLARA PUEBLO

Just south of Espanola, **the Santa Clara Pueblo's Puye Cliffs National Historic Landmark** is the ancestral home of the Santa Clara Pueblo. Dating back 1100 to 1580 AD, the site contains the cliff and cave dwellings of the Ancestral Puebloans.

Tourism in this area actually goes back to the early 1900s, when the AT&SF Railroad offered tours of the American Southwest. Fred Harvey offered his famous day trips throughout the area and constructed one of his stopping places at the pueblo. It remains the only Harvey House on a Native American reservation and is now the visitor center. Several

different tours are available. Reservations are highly recommended.
300 Highway 30
Santa Clara Pueblo, NM 87532
(888) 320-5008
http://www.puyecliffs.com

SANTA FE (SEE ALSO TESUQUE)

The capital city of New Mexico is also the nation's oldest capital, founded in the early years of the 1600s. It has a well-deserved international reputation as both a premiere art destination and a charming city. It's also supremely historic.

The video "Through the Lens: Imaging Santa Fe" shows some of the changes.
https://www.youtube.com/watch?v=HNa-1Tlrvu0

TRAILS THAT LINKED THE COUNTRY
Although the Santa Fe Trail is famous, trade through the Southwest had been ongoing for centuries. El Camino Real de Tierra Adentro, the Royal Road of the Interior, dates 200 years farther back to the early 1600s. Ending in San Juan Pueblo/Ohkay Owingeh New Mexico, the road reached down through Santa Fe to Mexico City and was the earliest Euro-American trade route in the United States—although native peoples had been trading up and down North America for far longer. Little is left to walk, but Agua Fria Street leads into the heart of Santa Fe, as it did when it was called El Camino Real.

With the El Camino Real route firmly in place, it was easy to create the linkage to the newer Santa Fe Trail. From the 1800s on, the Santa Fe Trail brought people and goods from Missouri to the territory of New Mexico via Santa Fe, straight into the city's historic plaza. The route is commemorated today by the National Park Service as the Santa Fe National Historic Trail.
http://www.nps.gov/safe/index.htm

Although time moved on, the history of Santa Fe Trail remains. Signs can be found throughout the city identifying parts of the road.

There is an outstanding sculpture at the entrance to Museum Hill off the Old Santa Fe Trail that celebrates that history. **Journey's End** by sculptor Reynaldo "Sonny" Rivera and landscape architect Richard Borkovetz is a bronze panorama that celebrates and honors the undaunted souls who made the journey. It is said that there are remnants of the trail's wagon ruts identified by an archaeological survey, but they aren't marked as such.

Whether or not we can see the ruts, exploring the sculpture puts us squarely on remnants of that famous and often perilous trail.

HISTORY AND ARCHITECTURE
Both tourists and residents love Santa Fe for its historic architecture. And this was totally by design. In 1958, prominent architect John Gaw Meem convinced the city to create zoning regulations that limited the style of the city's architecture for all new buildings. Although this restriction is now loosening up a bit, much of the historic part of the city's architecture is Pueblo Revival and Territorial with beautiful Spanish accents.

Pueblo Revival combined elements of the building styles used in construction of the pueblos of New Mexico—adobe bricks, flat roofs, wooden beams, and kiva, or rounded interior fireplaces. Spanish colonial designs, a popular style for churches, added elaborate facades and prominent belfries or bell towers. The Spanish also brought their love of courtyards, shutters, and fountains to the architectural mélange.

Territorial style, developed while New Mexico was transitioning from a territory to a state, included Greek Revival trim (usually painted white) over windows and doors and brick coping on the top of the walls. Often a covered walkway was added to the front of a building.

It is said that the emphasis on architectural homogeneity, along with its focus on local style, gave Santa Fe its nickname The City Different. Learn more about how the city acquired its nickname at: http://santafelibrary.blogspot.com/2007/06/refq-origin-of-our-city-different.html

SPECIAL FOCUS: JOHN GAW MEEM

John Gaw Meem was born into a missionary family in Brazil in 1894. He never had any formal architectural training. In fact, his degree was in Structural Engineering, and his experience included working in New York City on its burgeoning subway system. After serving in WWI and then becoming dissatisfied with engineering, Meem used his fluency in Portuguese to land a job as a banker in Rio de Janeiro.

But that job didn't last. Meem was diagnosed with tuberculosis and was brought back to New York City. In an interview, Meem recalls his discussion with his doctor. "'Now you can go to Saratoga or you can go to North Carolina or you could go to New Mexico. I know of a place in Santa Fe but,' he said, 'I think that you're going to have to be in bed a while.' Well, I walked out of there and on my way toward Broadway saw a big sign that said Santa Fe Railroad and I went over and asked them if they had any information about New Mexico or Santa Fe and I got this little pamphlet with a picture of the Museum of New Mexico which had just put up the Fine Arts Building and I got quite excited seeing that and pictures of Indian dances and I decided right then and there that I was coming here to New Mexico instead of going somewhere else."

(Quote Source: Oral history interview with John Gaw Meem, 1964 Dec. 3, Archives of American Art, Smithsonian Institution. http://www.aaa.si.edu/collections/interviews/oral-history-interview-john-gaw-meem-12968)

In 1920, Meem moved to Santa Fe and checked into one of the sanatoriums constructed to treat those with tuberculosis and asthma. He became captivated with New Mexican architecture.

When his treatment ended almost two years later, Meem headed up to Denver for formal training in architecture, but a relapse brought him back to Santa Fe. But bedrest didn't stop him from pursuing his goal of becoming an architect. Commissions flowed in and Meem designed estates for the wealthy in Pueblo Spanish style, sometimes with touches from New Mexico's Territorial period.

By 1928 he was Santa Fe's leading architect, known for his ability to interpret traditional design elements using modern materials. He used stucco instead of adobe bricks and added glass windows to allow light and air to enter. His remodeling of La Fonda Hotel in Santa Fe (1929) is legendary for his respectful updating of the original design.

He was asked to design the University of New Mexico's Administration Building (now the library) in 1936. It was so successfully received that for 26 years he was the architect for UNM.

Meem developed the architectural style now called Pueblo Revival, which became both prevalent and unique to the Southwest. Meem died in Santa Fe in 1983.

Today you can see his legacy in the evocative buildings throughout the Southwest. Some of his treasures in New Mexico include: Fuller Lodge, Los Alamos Ranch School, Los Alamos, NM (1928); Los Poblanos, Los Ranchos de Albuquerque (1932); Albuquerque Little Theatre, Albuquerque (1936); Maisel's Indian Trading Post, Albuquerque (1939), as well as many of the buildings on the University of New Mexico's Albuquerque campus.

One of the architectural and religious highlights of Santa Fe is the **Cathedral Basilica of Saint Francis of Assisi**. From the founding of the city in 1610, there has been a church in the same spot in Santa Fe. The first church was a modest adobe church, but within 20 years, it was replaced with a larger church to accommodate the growing population. That building was destroyed in the Pueblo Revolt of 1680 and was replaced in 1714 with a new building named in honor of Saint Francis of Assisi, the Patron Saint of Santa Fe.

In 1869, Santa Fe's first bishop, Father John Baptiste Lamy, built the present cathedral, which was completed in 1887. It was elevated to a basilica in 2005. When you gaze at this beautiful structure, you are gazing at 400 years of history.

According to the church's website, the only part of the original structure still remaining is the small adobe chapel dedicated to Our Lady La Conquistadora. Brought from Spain in 1625, the statue is said to be the oldest representation of the Virgin Mary in the United States.

Astute visitors might notice "Adonoi" inscribed in Hebrew over the front arch of the cathedral. There are two explanations for this, but neither is universally accepted.

One theory is that this inscription was put there by Archbishop Lamy to honor the Jewish friends and neighbors in Santa Fe who supported the constructed of the church. An alternative explanation is that a triangle with Jehovah or Yahweh (or in this case the Hebrew word for God, Adonoi) in the center is a symbol of the Holy Trinity.
131 Cathedral Place
Santa Fe, NM 87501
(505) 982-5619
http://www.cbsfa.org/

San Miguel Chapel is known in Santa Fe simply as "The Oldest Church" because it is claimed to be the oldest church in the continental United States. The earliest documentation available in support of the existence of San Miguel Chapel dates back to 1628, so it was likely built sometime before then. The church was partially destroyed during the Pueblo Revolt

of 1680. The present building dates back to 1710, although it has undergone significant changes over the last 200 years.
401 Old Santa Fe Trail
Santa Fe, NM 87501
(505) 982-3974
http://sanmiguelchapel.org/

La Fonda Hotel reigns over the heart of Santa Fe's historic Plaza. There has been lodging on that spot since the Spanish established the city in 1607. When intrepid travelers and merchants ended their journey along established trade routes, there was a fonda (inn) to greet them.

The current La Fonda was built in 1922 and acquired in 1925 by the Atchison, Topeka & Santa Fe Railway before being leased to Fred Harvey, who turned it into one of his famous Harvey Houses. Architect and designer Mary Jane Colter transformed the interior, as she did with many of his buildings.

The building changed, the owners changed, and even the name has changed, but there's still an inn on that site greeting travelers.
100 E San Francisco St.
Santa Fe, NM 87501
(505) 982-5511
http://www.lafondasantafe.com/

The **Lensic Theater** opened in 1931. As with many others historic theaters, it fell into disrepair and was rescued decades later, reopening in 2001 as a performing arts center hosting events including film festivals, concerts, and special events.
211 W San Francisco St.
Santa Fe, NM 87501
(505) 988-7050
https://www.lensic.org/

Santa Fe is also famous for its **Santa Fe Opera House**—perhaps the only open air opera house in the country. Located outside of the historic area, James Stewart Polshek and Partners were free to create an innovative, contemporary design. Ticket holders can enjoy a variety of tours and talks that are included in the ticket price. Backstage tours are also given Monday through Friday at 9:00 a.m.

301 Opera Drive
Santa Fe, NM 87506
(505) 986-5900
http://www.santafeopera.org/yourvisit/enhanceyourexperience/inde
x.aspx

WORLD WAR II

Although not touched directly by the events of World War II, the city nevertheless participated in some of the upheavals. Los Alamos was the New Mexico center of research and development. Even though all the staff had to be on site, no one could know where they were. In order to keep New Mexico's atomic city unknown, everyone's address was a **Santa Fe post office box**. Most scientists used PO Box 1663 as their mailing address. Today a plaque identifies the important role played by that the post office.
109 East Palace
Santa Fe, NM 87501
http://manhattanprojectvoices.org/location/santa-fe-nm

One of the sad chapters in New Mexico's history is the treatment of the Japanese-American citizens during World War II. After the attack on Pearl Harbor in December 1941, the US Government rounded up citizens of Japanese ancestry and forced them into **internment camps** across the country. One of these camps was in Santa Fe. From March 1942 until April 1946, the Santa Fe Interment Camp held over 4,000 people.

Today, a suburban park sits on the camp site. Frank Ortiz Park is known for its dog-friendly policies. But there is a memorial plaque reached by a paved path just to the left of the children's playground.
1160 Camino De Las Crucitas
Santa Fe, NM 87501
Cross Streets: Between La Loma Vis and Michelle Drive
(505) 955-2100

Those interested in military history will want to visit the **New Mexico National Guard Bataan Memorial Museum**. It is a tribute to the New Mexican veterans who were forced into the infamous Bataan Death March. Of the 1,800 who started, only

900 survived. Admission to this memorial museum is free, but donations are always welcome.
1050 Old Pecos Trail
Santa Fe, NM 87505
(505) 474-1670
http://www.bataanmuseum.com/

ART AND CULTURE

Despite having the oldest capitol building in the United States, it isn't the length of time the city has existed that lures visitors to Santa Fe. With its population of 70,000, it is one of the most significant art cities in the world, and is said to have the highest number of artists per capita (although the artists in Taos may disagree).

There are art galleries on every street and around every corner. The city hosts over 200 galleries and several stellar art fairs including Indian Market, Spanish Market, and the International Folk Art Market, which bring in collectors and spectators from around the world.

Even the state capitol building, known as the **Roundhouse** (it is the only round state house in the country), overflows with art—around 600 paintings, photographs, sculptures, and more are on display inside. Plus, there are over six acres of grounds filled with even more art. Tours of the building are given regularly, but check the website for the exact schedule.
Old Santa Fe Trail and Paseo de Peralta.
411 State Capitol
Santa Fe, NM 87501
(505) 986-4589
http://www.nmlegis.gov/lcs/visitors.aspx

CANYON ROAD

In a city filled with galleries and artists, Canyon Road still stands out by offering a unique art-filled experience. If you've ever thought how much fun it would be to window-shop for art, to chat with gallery owners and artists, to poke around in a treasure trove of pottery, paintings, watercolor, sculpture, and almost every creative product you can imagine, Canyon Road is your destination. Over half the galleries in the city line its half-mile length.
http://visitcanyonroad.com/

If you get hungry, tired, or thirsty, take a break with a cup of tea or a light meal at **The Tea House**, and you can buy some of their amazing teas in bulk to take home.
821 Canyon Road
Santa Fe, NM 87501
(505) 992-0972
http://teahousesantafe.com/

Allan Houser Gallery and Sculpture Gardens
Born Allan C. Haozous, this sculptural artist and his family led a convulsive life. His parents, Sam and Blossom Haozous, were members of the Chiricahua Apache tribe. When members of the tribe refused to leave their lands and relocate to Arizona, 1,200 Chiricahuas were sent by cattle-car train to internment facilities. As a child, Sam Haozous was held in Castillo de San Marcos in St. Augustine. Blossom was born in Mount Vernon Barracks, Alabama.

Eventually many of the Chiricahuas were relocated to Oklahoma. Sam and Blossom choose to stay in that area when they were finally freed in 1914. They also changed their name to Houser. Allan was born just months after their release.

Houser grew up farming, but his real love was art. In 1934 he enrolled in the art program at the Santa Fe Indian School. Within five years, his work was being shown around the country. Houser eventually moved to Santa Fe and is credited with one thousand sculptures in stone, wood, and bronze. He was a major figure on the international art scene until his death in 1994.

You can find his work in Santa Fe at the **Allan Houser Gallery**.
125 Lincoln Ave.
Santa Fe, NM 87501
(505) 982-4705
http://www.allanhouser.com/

Guided tours of his sculpture garden are also available. Reservations are required. Call to schedule a tour of his home studio and sculpture garden, which has eighty-five outdoor pieces on ten acres.
22 Haozous Road

Santa Fe, NM 87508
(505) 471-1528
http://www.allanhouser.com/index.php/sculpture-garden/sculpture-garden-sales-and-tours

The **School for Advanced Research (SAR)** is a relatively unknown gem. It started in 1907 as the School of American Archaeology, but its scope widened over the years to include Native American art and a diversity of interests that simply defy classification.

SAR offers several lectures each year that can include such varied topics as human evolution, animal emotions of love and grief, and archeology.

They also have a large collection of over 12,000 pieces of Native American art, including pottery, jewelry, textiles and clothing, paintings, basketry, and drums. Visitors can tour the collection but reservations are required.

SAR also offers Walking History Tours of the eight-acre estate, formerly known as "El Delirio" (The Madness), which was the home of wealthy socialites, Amelia Elizabeth White and Martha Root White, in the 1920s. These tours are not regularly scheduled, and SAR recommends calling in advance.
660 Garcia St.
Santa Fe, NM 87505
(505) 954-7205

Santa Fe also has a cutting-edge side. Formed in 2008 as an art collective, Meow Wolf specializes in groundbreaking art initiatives. They describe themselves as an arts production company that creates immersive, multimedia experiences that transport audiences of all ages into fantastic realms of storytelling. That mission and their installations put them on the very edge of contemporary art.

They have gained a patron in George RR Martin (the author of the A Song of Ice and Fire series, which eventually became the HBO television series, Game of Thrones). He purchased and renovated a 33,000 square foot building on 2.6 acres of land and leased it back to Meow Wolf for 10 years. The innovative art collective then created its first permanent exhibit, **House**

of Eternal Return. Visitors are invited to walk, climb, and crawl through a labyrinth of a Victorian mansion. Over 130 artists were involved in its creation.
1352 Rufina Circle
Santa Fe, NM 87507
(505) 395-6369
https://meowwolf.com/

MUSEUMS
As the capital city, Santa Fe is home to several important museums. At the time the city was founded, the Palace of Governors was built as Spain's governmental seat in its new territory. Later, in 1846, when the United States declared New Mexico an American territory, the Palace became the territorial capitol, and for a time the building was the state capitol building.

Although it is considered the oldest public building still in existence in the United States, its appearance has changed over the centuries. It has also been seized at least twice. First from 1680-1693 during the Pueblo Revolt (See Special Focus: Pueblo Revolt of 1680), and then again by the Confederacy in 1862 during the Civil War.

Today, the architecture is Spanish Pueblo Revival with Territorial elements. Perhaps with a touch of humor, the National Park Service has referred to the **Palace of Governors** as the largest artifact of the New Mexico History Museum. Free docent-led tours are available.
105 W Palace Ave.
Santa Fe, NM 87501
(505) 478-5100
http://www.nps.gov/nr/travel/american_latino_heritage/Palace_of_the _Governors.html

Located next to the Palace of Governors on the Plaza, the New **Mexico History Museum** is arguably the finest history museum in the state. Opened in 2009, this modern interpretation of an adobe building reveals the diversity of New Mexico's complex history through huge-scale photographs and interactive displays. One of the most engaging aspects of the museum is the way it represents the history of the state—told through people's lives, thus adding a human dimension to the often chaotic panorama of events.

Don't miss the Segesser Hide Paintings created to depict events in the early 1700s. The hides themselves are on display at the Palace of Governors, but there's an interactive kiosk in the history museum. They are amazing and so is their history. You can also explore them online:
http://www.nmhistorymuseum.org/hides/
105 W Palace Ave.
Santa Fe, NM 87501
(505) 476-5100
http://www.nmhistorymuseum.org/

The Palace of Governors and the New Mexico History Museum are part of the Museum of New Mexico system focused on Santa Fe. In addition to these, there are three other museums sponsored by New Mexico.

New Mexico Museum of Art offers art walking tours of Santa Fe from April to November, highlighting the art and architectural history of downtown Santa Fe. They also offer several long-term exhibits each year.
107 West Palace Ave.
Santa Fe, NM 87501
(505) 476-5072
http://www.nmartmuseum.org/

Museum Hill hosts several of the city's finest museums. Two of the museums are part of the New Mexico History Museum system—the Museum of International Folk Art and the Museum of Indian Arts and Culture. In addition, Museum Hill hosts the Museum of Spanish Colonial Art and the Wheelwright Museum of the American Indian. As the name suggests, it's located on a hill overlooking town. You can follow the signs or set your GPS to find the intersection of Camino Lejo and Camino Corrales.

The Museum of Contemporary Native Arts is the country's only museum with a focus on the new dimensions and directions of Native American artists. It's located on the Plaza.
108 Cathedral Place
Santa Fe, NM 87501

(888) 922-4242
http://www.iaia.edu/museum/

Georgia O'Keeffe Museum is devoted to the work of O'Keeffe and those she influenced as well as artists who were her contemporaries. It is the largest collection of O'Keeffe's work in the world and includes 1,149 O'Keeffe paintings, drawings, and sculptures that date from 1901 to 1984 (the year she retired from painting). Take a docent-led tour to learn her history as an artist and peek into her life. It adds a crucial dimension to O'Keeffe, fleshing her out as a person and an artist. (See Special Focus: Georgia O'Keeffe.)
217 Johnson St.
Santa Fe, NM 87501
(505) 946-1000
http://www.okeeffemuseum.org/

Just south of Santa Fe is the living history museum of El **Rancho de las Golondrinas.** The site shelters original buildings from the early 1700s and reconstructed buildings from other parts of northern New Mexico.
334 Los Pinos Road
Santa Fe, NM 87507
(505) 471-2261
http://www.golondrinas.org/

CREATIVE SANTA FE
Not only can you view a cornucopia of art in Santa Fe, you can participate in it as well. In fact, one of the coolest things to do in Santa Fe is to become an artist yourself. The creatives of the city have put together art workshops and other hands-on experiences. If you can think of a possible activity, chances are that someone is offering it.
http://santafe.org/Visiting_Santa_Fe/Things_to_Do/Classes_and_Workshops/index.html

Porcelain sculptor, **Heidi Loewen**, offers private lessons and small group workshops. She takes throwing pots and platters on the wheel to a new level of art. She's also developed some very special techniques that she shares with participants. At the end, Heidi will fire your creations and ship them to you (or you can pick them up if you're local).

69

315 Johnson St.
Santa Fe, NM 87501
(505) 988-2225
http://www.heidiloewen.com/

DRINKING AND COOKING

Santa Fe Spirits is a distillery that not only produces a heavenly gin but also offers almost a half dozen varieties of spirits. Started by Colin Keegan in 2010, Santa Fe Spirits is justly proud of their award-winning Colkegan Single Malt Whiskey, which won Gold as one of the best American whiskies at the Ultimate Spirits Challenge. Mesquite-smoked grain gives this sipping whiskey a unique Southwest smokiness. Tours of the distillery are available.
7505 Mallard Way Unit I
Santa Fe, NM 87507
(505) 467-8892
Book the fee-based tour online at
https://a.zozi.com/#/express/santafespiritsnm/products/64189

Santa Fe School of Cooking offers an array of three-hour Southwest cooking workshops and classes. In a city with almost as many restaurants as galleries, visitors can also enjoy their restaurant walking tours.
125 N Guadalupe St.
Santa Fe, NM 87501
(800) 982-4688
(505) 983-4511
http://santafeschoolofcooking.com/

Santa Fe Culinary Academy offers a one-year Professional Culinary Program, but for visitors to the city, they also have one-day community cooking classes as well as fun and distinctive pop-up restaurants. These unique pop-ups are usually held the first Thursday of each month. Of course, if you're a more serious chef, they also offer classes that last several days.
112 W San Francisco St.
Suite 300
Santa Fe, NM 87501
(505) 983-7445
http://www.santafeculinaryacademy.com/

TAOS (SEE ALSO RANCHOS DE TAOS AND TAOS PUEBLO)

Taos is another art epicenter of New Mexico with an outsize art presence, given its population of just under 6,000.

As with so many towns in New Mexico, Native Americans were there first—this time in the form of the Taos Pueblo, containing buildings said to date back to 1100 AD. It vies with the Acoma Pueblo for appellation of the oldest continuous settlement in North America.

The Spanish history of Taos starts in 1540, when Capitan Hernando Alvarado (part of the expedition of Francisco Vasquez de Coronado) arrived in the Taos Valley. When Don Juan de Onate began establishing colonies under the Spanish, Taos officially became a Spanish village.

It didn't take long for the heavy-handed invaders to foment rebellion. The Spanish demanded tribute from the population, and the missionaries sought to save them from their heathen ways. Neither went over well with the independent Pueblo. In 1640, the people of the Taos Pueblo successfully but temporarily revolted. Eventually the Spanish did return (in 1661); however, that didn't end the hostilities. The Pueblo Revolt was in progress in 1680, and the Taos Pueblo joined the rebellion. This, too, didn't last, and the Spanish came back with the Spanish Reconquest of 1692. That still didn't end the hostilities with the Taos Pueblo, who continued their resistance until 1696. (See Special Focus: Popé's Rebellion/Pueblo Revolt.)

About 200 years later, far more benevolent invaders came to Taos, the result of a wagon breakdown. In 1898, artists Bert Phillips and Ernest Blumenschein had a mishap with their conveyance and had to stop to have their wagon wheel repaired. They fell in love with the mountains and the light (which is quite extraordinary), and stayed. They eventually formed the Taos Society of Artists, which started the great migration of artists to Taos.

In the 1950s, Ski Taos opened and created another migration, this time of skiers visiting the slopes each winter. Shortly after that, the counterculture revolution brought hippies who wanted to live more natural and off-the-grid lives.

All these invasions, whether benign or military, make for a diverse mix of residents and unique experiences for visitors. But what also adds to the piquancy of a visit to Taos is the whiff (or perhaps a full-fledge wind) of scandal.

THE STORIES OF TAOS

Taos is a city of stories, and some scandalous. *Mabel Dodge Luhan*, whose complete name would be **Mabel Ganson Evans Dodge Sterne Luhan**, was the heiress of a Buffalo family. She found love in Taos in 1918 when she met Tony Luhan, of the Taos Pueblo. Mabel actually started out in Santa Fe a year earlier to join her third husband, Maurice Sterne, but shortly after they moved to Taos, she and Maurice were divorced. When Mabel met Tony Luhan, things began to heat up. Luhan was, inconveniently, married at the time, but in 1923 Mabel managed to marry Luhan anyway.

With a handsome Native husband (from the Taos Pueblo) and plenty of heiress money, Mabel created a circle of famous artists and writers. Literary and artistic luminaries such as D.H. Lawrence, Georgia O'Keeffe, Ansel Adams, and more visited her large, eclectic home. In fact, Ansel Adams took a quite famous photo of Tony Luhan in 1930 (it's owned by Ansel Adams Publishing Rights Trust and cannot be reproduced).

Mabel died in August 1962 and is said to have been buried in the extreme southwest corner of Kit Carson Cemetery in Taos. Tony died less than six months later in January 1963 and is buried back in the old cemetery at the Taos Pueblo.

The house has gone through several transformation and reinventions, but the **Mabel Dodge Luhan House** is currently a B&B and historic landmark.
240 Morada Lane
Taos, NM 87571
(800) 846-2235
(575) 751-9686
http://mabeldodgeluhan.com/

D.H. Lawrence, perhaps best known for his once-scandalous book, Lady Chatterley's Lover, also lived for a time in the area around Taos and, in a sense, is still there.

As part of her quest to be a major arts patron, Mabel Luhan definitely wanted to lure D.H. Lawrence to live in New Mexico as part of her inner circle of writers and artists. 3Luhan herself was a force of nature that few could resist. She was so keen to keep Lawrence in Taos that she actually created a retreat for him and his wife that ultimately became the D.H. Lawrence Ranch.

Lawrence, his wife Frieda, and artist-friend Dorothy Brett did stay at the ranch. Despite having a house on the grounds, the Lawrences actually spent very little time there. It was Dorothy Brett who really lived there, in a tiny cabin with sweeping views amidst the woods.

The D.H. Lawrence Ranch, about 20 miles north of Taos in San Cristobal, has been reopened to visitors, currently on a limited summer-only schedule. It is also the site of the D.H. Lawrence Memorial. If you do visit, be prepared for all manner of fascinating bits of gossip. The stories alone are worth the trip to the ranch.

Take NM 522 north and turn right at the D.H. Lawrence Historic Marker. Follow the road and stay on the right. http://www.friendsofdhlawrence.org/

Lawrence has another connection to Taos. Some of his paintings hang at the **Hotel La Fonda de Taos** on the Plaza in historic Taos as the **Forbidden Art Collection**, and it was quite a convoluted journey.

The nine paintings were originally part of an exhibition of 13 that was confiscated by the police from a London gallery in 1929 after being deemed obscene. The paintings, neither exceedingly scandalous nor particularly good, were in danger of being destroyed until Lawrence managed to remove them from England. Shortly after Frieda's death, her then current husband sold or gave them to Sake Karavas, who was the owner of the Hotel La Fonda de Taos.

73

They hung in Karavas' office until he died in 1996. The paintings and the hotel moved on to his longtime friends, George and Cordy Sahd. The Sahds still own the hotel and the paintings. They are now displayed in a separate art-filled room, hidden from view by a curtain. For a fee, the paintings are revealed and visitors can receive a briefing on them.
108 S Plaza
Taos, NM 87571
(575) 758-2211
http://www.lafondataos.com/

The **Taos Center for the Arts** is a museum and art gallery, but the building was once the home of one of the town's true villains, **Arthur Manby.** He had acquired much of the land by less than honest measures, including using suspicious land grants to take the property away from the local families. In 1929, Manby was found dead in his home, minus his head (which might or might not have been found in another room, reports are vague about this). The crime was never solved and his death was never mourned.
133 Paseo del Pueblo Norte
Taos, NM 87571
(575) 758-2052
http://tcataos.org/

Doc Martin was as loved as Manby was hated. Dr. Thomas Paul (Doc) Martin came to Taos in the 1890s and bought the largest of several adobe houses that surrounded a small plaza. His wife, Helen Martin, was an artist and sister-in-law to Bert Phillips, one of the founding fathers of the art community. Gradually, the Martins bought the other buildings around the plaza and rented them to writers and artists.

When Doc died, Helen bought the last remaining building that enclosed the plaza and formally opened the Hotel Martin in 1936. Later, owners changed the name to the **Taos Inn**, but this charming collection of buildings, named to the State Register of Historic Places, is still a Taos hub and landmark. Stop by to listen to the music and have a drink in the Adobe Bar, enjoy a meal in Doc Martin's Restaurant, and wander through history.
125 Paseo Del Pueblo Norte
Taos, NM 87571
(575) 758-2233
http://www.taosinn.com/

Although most artists who found their way to Taos were from the United States, **Nicolai Fechin** was a Russian artist who arrived in 1927 with his wife Alexandra and daughter Eya in hopes the climate would be beneficial for his tuberculosis. Fechin bought an adobe home and completely renovated it into a piece of art.

The combination of adobe structure and Russian wood carvings has made the house, now a museum open to the public, one of the most unusual and beautiful homes in Taos. It is absolutely worth a visit.
227 Paseo Del Pueblo Norte
Taos, NM 87571
(575) 758-2690
http://www.taosartmuseum.org/fechin.html

Another player in the drama of Taos history was **Kit Carson.** He was a trapper, guide, Indian agent, and Army officer. He is, depending on who you talk to, an object of hatred, sympathy, or even honor. His first two wives were from the Arapahoe and Cheyenne tribes. After his second marriage ended, Carson married the 14-year-old daughter of a prominent Taos family.

In 1843, he bought an adobe house that is now the **Kit Carson Museum.** It has guided tours and a nice video about his life. Definitely take the tour to learn more about his life and times. (See Special Focus: Christopher Kit Carson)
113 Kit Carson Rd.
Taos, NM 87571
(575)758-4945
http://www.kitcarsonhomeandmuseum.com

Although Carson died in Colorado in 1868, his body was brought back to Taos, where he was laid to rest in the park that now bears his name—the **Kit Carson Park and Historic Cemetery.**
211 Paseo Del Pueblo Norte
Taos, NM 87571

SPECIAL FOCUS: CHRISTOPHER KIT CARSON

The controversy over whether Kit Carson was a friend or foe of the Native Americans stems from the complexity of the man and his role in the Long Walk of the Navajo. Carson was born in Missouri in 1809 and was apprenticed to a saddlemaker when he was 14. He didn't have the temperament for that occupation and soon headed out to Santa Fe, and Taos.

Carson was a scout, fur-trapper, and explorer who spoke Spanish and French in addition to English. He fought in both the Mexican-American War and for the Union in the Civil War. He became a legendary figure in the Wild West. In terms of his beliefs, heart, and soul, far less is known.

Carson's first wife was Arapahoe. There's a very sweet, but unsubstantiated story about their "courtship." It was the summer of 1836 and a rather boorish French trapper was pursuing an Arapaho girl named Waanibe (also known as Alice). A duel followed and Carson won both the duel and the woman. They had one daughter, Adaline. Sadly, in 1840, Alice died giving birth to a second child. Even less is known of his next wife, other than she was Cheyenne and she divorced him by dumping his belongings and Adaline outside their home.

In 1843, Kit Carson married Josefa Jaramillo, the 14-year-old daughter of a wealthy and influential Taos family.

His treatment of Native Americans made Carson controversial. He strongly supported the US government's annex of Indian land in the Southwest. When the Navajo refused to leave their tribal land, Carson began a program to destroy their crops, orchards, and livestock. As history shows, the Navajo lost and began the Long Walk to Fort Sumner, New Mexico. Many died along the way.

Up until that point, from 1854 to 1861, Carson served as an Indian Agent, a mediator between the different tribes and the United States government, largely because he was felt to be fair and sympathetic to the Native population. However, he was never pro-Indian—only distinguishing between those he worked with and those he fought. Although there is some evidence that he did plead the case of the Navajo, it is certain that he waged a no-holds-barred war against them.

HISTORICAL LANDMARKS

The **Old Courthouse**, located on the north side of the plaza, was built in 1934 in Spanish-Pueblo style, giving it a rather friendly look from the outside. Today, there are art galleries on the ground floor and the remains of the old jail.

Go up to the second floor to see part of the original courthouse. Its Works Progress Administration (WPA) murals depict aspects of the theme of social justice and were restored in 1995.
104 North Plaza
Taos, NM 87571
http://oldcountycourthouse.com/index.php

The **Harwood Museum of Art,** founded in 1923, is the second oldest art museum in the state after the New Mexico Museum of Art in Santa Fe. It contains seven galleries of historic and contemporary art, plus temporary exhibits by Taos artists.
238 Ledoux St.
Taos, NM 87571
(575) 758-9826
http://www.harwoodmuseum.org/

In 1947, Millicent Rogers came to Taos. She was the granddaughter of one of the founders of the Standard Oil Company and had the financial ability to pursue her passions. One of her passions was Southwest art—pottery, jewelry, kachina figures, rugs, and baskets. **The Millicent Rogers Museum** exhibits her collections.
1504 Millicent Rogers Road
El Prado, NM 87529
(575) 758-2462
http://www.millicentrogers.org/

Ernest Blumenschein, one of the two founders of the art movement in Taos, eventually moved permanently to Taos with his wife and daughter. Their home became the **Blumenschein Home and Museum**. It is maintained the way

77

it was in the early 1900s and showcases the family collection of art and antiques.
222 Ledoux St.
Taos, NM 87571
(575) 758-0505
http://taoshistoricmuseums.org/

No description of Taos would be complete without the hacienda built by Severino Martin (later Martinez) circa 1804. The **Hacienda de los Martinez** is one of the few Great Houses that remains from the Late Spanish Colonial period. It was built in two sections, each around its own courtyard or placita. The building has been maintained the way the Martinez family would have used it, and visitors are encouraged to wander through the rooms. There's also a blacksmith shop, kitchen, and grande sala for parties. It is now part of Taos Historic Museums, and its authenticity and location makes it a favorite with photographers.
708 Hacienda Road at NM 240
Taos, NM 87571
(575) 758-1000
http://www.taoshistoricmuseums.org

One of the more stunning sights in Taos is the **Rio Grande Gorge Bridge** that spans the Rio Grande from a height of over 500 feet. It's one of the highest bridges in the United States and provides striking views of the river and the cliffs below. The bridge is located several miles outside of Taos on Route 64.

The hippies who moved to Taos brought with them a desire to live off the grid. That meant using as little electricity and non-renewable energy sources as possible. The result is a **solar radio station** and some very green housing.

Founded by Brad Hockmeyer, Radio station KTAO sends out a signal on 100 percent solar power. It is now owned by several former employees and includes the KTAOS Solar Center music venue and a full-service bar and restaurant.
9 State Road 150
Taos, NM 87571
(575) 758-5826
http://ktao.com/blog

Taos' **Earthships** are solar houses built from natural and recycled materials, and there is nothing standard about their architecture. These homes are available to rent for the night or the week. There's a tour of the Earthship Visitor Center (self-guided and fee-based) with staff on hand to answer questions. If you're interested in learning how to construct an Earthship, workshops are available.
#2 Earthship Way
Tres Piedras, NM 87577
http://earthship.com/visit-us

TAOS PUEBLO (SEE ALSO TAOS)

The Acoma and Taos Pueblos are the two oldest continuously settled communities in the United States. Taos is also considered to be the largest surviving multistoried pueblo structure in the US. Its sprawling adobe blocks piled several stories high make it visually stunning and a photographer favorite. It's also open to visitors, but there is an additional fee if you want to take photographs.

The **Taos Pueblo** is on the National Register of Historic Places as well as on the United National World Heritage List. But what makes Taos Pueblo special is that it is very much a living pueblo where the people go about their daily lives, baking bread in the horno ovens, doing maintenance on the adobe, selling jewelry and pottery in some of the tiny rooms of the pueblo.

The pueblo even has its own water supply. The Rio Pueblo flows down from the sacred Blue Lake and into the pueblo, where it is used for drinking water and irrigation of crops.

Visitors who begin to chat with some of the older members of the pueblo might discover that the people have a particular fondness for Richard Nixon. There is a story behind this unusual affection for a politician. It was Nixon who signed into law the bill that returned the Blue Lake and 48,000 acres of land to the pueblo, which had been seized by the US government in 1933.

Guided tours of the pueblo are available. Although not required, they add a vital historical and cultural component to your visit. Otherwise, you're just admiring the striking architecture and the lovely San Geronimo Church, built in 1850 (which replaced the original church built in 1619).
120 Veterans Highway
Taos, NM 87571
(575) 758-1028
http://taospueblo.com/

Enjoy the video flyover tour of the Taos Pueblo:
https://youtu.be/BBPAiX6MmzE

TESUQUE (SEE ALSO SANTA FE)

There are two Tesuques near Santa Fe. There is the Tesuque Pueblo, but there is also a separate town named Tesuque.

Small in terms of population but not in terms of land, the Tesuque Pueblo is home to less than 1,000 people across 17,000 acres. The pueblo operates the seasonal "destination" **Tesuque Flea Market** just off Highway 84/285.

15 Flea Market Road
Santa Fe, NM 87506
(505) 670-2599
http://www.pueblooftesuquefleamarket.com/

There are two remarkable art-related destinations in the town of Tesuque, located just five miles north of Santa Fe. The **Shidoni Foundry** and Galleries is likely the only place in the state which combines outdoor sculpture gardens with an active foundry that is open to the public.

The name Shidoni is derived from the Navajo greeting to a friend, and this amiable place lives up to that name. The galleries are generally open until 5:00 p.m. Self-guided foundry tours are only available Monday through Friday from noon to 1:00 p.m. while the foundry shuts down for lunch. If you can make it, the public is invited to watch an actual pour on Saturdays starting at noon, but they advise calling to verify the actual start time.
1508 Bishops Lodge Road
Tesuque, NM 87574
(505) 988-8001
http://www.shidoni.com/html/home.asp

Located next door, **Tesuque Glassworks** highlights two forms of glass. It's not hard to find blown glass studios, but Charlie Miner's studio also creates unique cast glass pieces. The procedure is a bit like the lost wax technique. The artist carves wax into the desired form, makes a mold, and then fills the mold with powdered glass. The process itself takes weeks to complete but the results are astonishing. The Santa Fe area has many glass artists, but Charlie Miner's Tesuque Glassworks is the most accessible to the public and the only one focused on this unique glass form. Open daily, seven days a week from 9:00 a.m. to 5:00 p.m.
1510 Bishops Lodge Road
Tesuque, NM 87574
(505) 988-2165
http://www.tesuqueglass.com/

TRUCHAS

The tiny town of Truchas on the High Road to Taos is famous for the 1988 movie, The Milagro Beanfield War (Miracle Bean Field War), which was directed by Robert Redford. It's a wonderful fable that highlights the importance of water to a town's survival. Villages across New Mexico have withered from a lack of water. If you loved the movie, it's worth a detour.

VELARDE

The town of Velarde, on the Low Road to Taos, is home to **Black Mesa Winery** and a good place to take a break and sample some wines.
1502 Highway 68 (MM 15)
Velarde, NM 87582
(505) 852.2820
http://www.blackmesawinery.com

NORTHEAST

Although most of the Enchanted Circle is in the North Central region, some of the towns on that loop are in fact, in the Northeast. If you plan to drive the area, you will likely be visiting both sections of the state.

CIMARRON

This Old West town lies about thirty minutes west of Eagle Nest on Route 64. While not exactly part of the Enchanted Circle, the road to reach Cimarron goes through the spectacular Cimarron Canyon State Park in the Colin Neblett Wildlife Area and is every bit as gorgeous as the traditional Enchanted Circle vistas. There are numerous pullouts and spots to park for hiking, picnics, and wildlife viewing. The starkly beautiful upthrust rock formations known as the Palisades are a great photo op and a destination for rock climbers.
http://www.emnrd.state.nm.us/SPD/cimarroncanyonstatepark.html

The main reason to visit Cimarron, apart from the beautiful drive, is the elegantly historic **St. James Hotel**, built in 1872. A visit to the hotel is a stroll back in time. The décor and architecture brings back the Old West. The only thing missing is the gunfights, although the bar is rumored to still have bullet holes in its pressed tin ceiling from the frequent gun battles.

The St. James sits on what now appears to be a quiet rural road, but South Collison Avenue has history—it was part of the famous Santa Fe Trail and was a stopping point for travelers and outlaws. Opened originally as a saloon by former chef to Abraham Lincoln, Henri Lambert, the business was so successful that a hotel was soon added.

Visitors can explore some of the rooms on the ground level, see the old photos, and read about the famous and infamous lodgers—a Who's Who of the Old West with Annie Oakley, Kit Carson, Frank and Jesse James, Wyatt Earp (and wife), Billy the Kid, and Black Jack Ketchum (See Clayton, New Mexico).

As it has done for almost 150 years, the St. James still welcomes lodgers. If you do plan on staying, call in advance. The hotel is a popular place. Although it doesn't offer tours, there are videos shown in the hotel lobby upon request (if they aren't already running).

You'll have no difficulty finding the St. James Hotel. There's a huge sign and right turn arrow at the corner of NM 64 and South Collison Avenue.
617 South Collison Ave.
Cimarron, NM 87714
(575) 376-2664
http://www.exstjames.com

The historic buildings in Cimarron along East 9th Street are home to some local businesses. Other historic sites include the **Colfax County Jail** from 1872 and the **Old Aztec Grist Mill Museum** built in 1864. The museum's hours are erratic and it is best to call the town's Visitor Center.

Cimarron's official historic district is located south of US Route 64 on the east and west sides of New Mexico Highway 21. In 1973, the district was added to the United States National

Register of Historic Places. According to the National Register, the district contains several significant buildings.

Make sure to stop by the **Visitor Center** for more information.
104 N. Lincoln Ave.
Cimarron, NM 87714
(575) 376-2417
http://www.cimarronnm.com/visitor-center.html

One of the most coveted and challenging of the Boy Scout camps is **Philmont Scout Ranch** on land donated by Waite and Genevieve Phillips (think Phillips 66 oil money). No small landowner, at one time they had over 300,000 acres. The Phillips began donating the land to the Boy Scouts between 1939 and 1941. The family named the sprawling acreage the Philmont Ranch—"Phil" for Phillips and "mont" for monte, the Spanish word for mountain. Their **Villa Philmonte** Spanish Mediterranean summer home on the ground of the Ranch is open for guided tours spring, summer, and fall. Call for dates and times.
7 Deer Run Road
Cimarron, NM 87714
(575) 376-1136
http://www.philmontscoutranch.org/Museums/Villa.aspx

CLAYTON

Clayton was a Santa Fe Trail town that thrived from the stream of goods making its way across the country. It continued as a railroad town, performing much the same function—a stopping point for merchandise traveling west. In fact, it was the appearance of the Colorado and Southern line that led to the founding of Clayton in 1888. This was also ranching territory, and the town soon boomed as a shipping center for cattle and wool. But Clayton boasts far more ancient history— dinosaurs and dinosaur tracks.

Visitors can explore the prehistoric dinosaur tracks at **Clayton Lake.** Established in the mid- 1950s to provide a habitat for migrating waterfowl, visitors today can not only indulge in birdwatching, but can also engage in a bit of dinosaur track viewing. Over 500 tracks from several types of dinosaurs can be seen from a boardwalk on the dam's spillway.

141 Clayton Lake Road
Clayton, NM 88415
(575) 374-8808
http://www.emnrd.state.nm.us/SPD/claytonlakestatepark.html

As a boomtown, Clayton boasted the **Luna**, a historic theater built in 1916 by merchant and rancher Morris Herzstein. The Mission Revival architecture of the building was tinkered with in the 1930s to add Art Deco fixtures and a marquee with an adorable winking neon moon face.

As with all historic buildings, there were financial challenges. Upgrades were needed, and normal maintenance was required. But with the enthusiastic efforts of volunteers, the theater was revitalized. In 2007, the Luna was listed on the United States National Register of Historic Places. The Town of Clayton purchased the theater from its former owners, the Leightons, and is bringing the theater technologically into the twenty-first century while preserving its beautiful architecture. The Luna Theater is one of New Mexico's oldest movie houses.
4 Main St.
Clayton, NM 88415
(575) 374-2712
http://www.claytonluna.com/

The other noteworthy historic building is actually just across the street from the theater. The 1892 **Eklund Hotel** with its sandstone façade still welcomes guests.
15 Main St.
Clayton, NM 88415
(575) 446-1939
Toll Free (888) 265-4683
http://hoteleklund.com/

Herzstein Memorial Museum started life in 1987 as the Union County Historical. As with many old buildings, the need for renovation outstripped the funding available. But there was history in the town that brought in outside funding, in this case from the Herzstein family.

Morris Herzstein had come to the United States from Germany in 1887 and originally settled in Liberty, New Mexico (a town that disappeared when the railroad bypassed it). But when his brother Levi was killed by outlaws, Morris moved to Clayton (See Special Focus: The Outlaw Black Jack Ketchum). The Herzstein family eventually migrated to Texas, where the family started the Albert and Ethel Herzstein Foundation. When the Clayton museum needed money, the foundation underwrote the cost of renovation and the museum was renamed in appreciation.

The museum displays items of daily life in historic Clayton donated by the community. While many towns have fascinating historical museums, this one includes themed collections rarely found elsewhere, including the largest Jim Deam saddle collection in the United States. J.H. Deam was a saddlemaker born and trained in Texas who moved to Clayton. In 1928, he went into business for himself making Western stock saddles, which have been described as real works of art. The museum also houses the largest WPA collection of furniture, pottery, paintings, and rugs made by those artisans in the state of New Mexico.

Admission is free but donations are appreciated.
22 S 2nd St.
Clayton, NM 88415
(575)374-2977
http://www.herzsteinmuseum.com/

SPECIAL FOCUS: THE OUTLAW BLACK JACK KETCHUM

Brothers Tom and Sam Ketchum, infamous train robbers in the late 1800s, had an important Clayton (and Herzstein) connection. The story starts down the road in the long-gone town of Liberty, New Mexico. According to historical accounts, the Ketchums rode in to buy supplies. When they returned that evening, they were caught in a thunderstorm and the store owners Morris and Levi Herzstein provided them with shelter, a kind gesture that would be repaid by theft and ultimately death.

When Levi Herzstein opened the store the next morning, he discovered they had been robbed by the Ketchum brothers. The Herzsteins gathered a small posse and went after them, but in the shootout that followed, Levi Herzstein and posse member

Hermenejildo Gallegos were killed. One surviving member, Placido Gurulé, provided an account reporting that he had been struck by a .30-30 bullet and knocked off his horse, so he survived Ketchum's attempt to murder any survivors.

According to Outlaw Tales of New Mexico: True Stories of New Mexico's Most Infamous by Barbara Marriott, there was no proof that the Ketchums perpetrated the murder until several years later, when Gurulé was said to have spotted Tom Ketchum at a Las Vegas, New Mexico train station. Although he identified him as one of the outlaws, nothing happened, and Tom and Sam simply left town to form the Black Jack Gang, pursuing train robbing, which was a far more lucrative business. Like many outlaws of the time, they headed to Cimarron and the St. James Hotel when they wanted a bit of a respite.

Finally, US Marshalls and local sheriffs formed a posse of skilled lawmen. A shootout ensued and Sam Ketchum was injured. He was eventually brought to a prison in Santa Fe, where he died of his wounds a few days later.

Apparently, Jack had not gotten word of these events because less than one month later, he went to rob one of his favorite train targets. But this time the conductor, likely fed up with multiple robberies, was armed and ready and blew off Black Jack's right arm. Although that didn't stop the crazy train robber from escaping, he was nonetheless captured, had the remains of his arm amputated, and sentenced to hang.

Black Jack Ketchum was hung in Clayton, New Mexico. But there is a bit of a coda. Due either to the hangman's inexperience or to being overly zealous, the rope used actually severed Ketchum's head instead of strangling him. A popular postcard showed the body—with its head sitting nearby. Morris Herzstein was reportedly present in Clayton to witness the hanging in 1901. Ketchum was buried in the cemetery in Clayton, where today tourists can take pictures of his headstone—or even perhaps a selfie.

CLEVELAND

The **Cleveland Roller Mill Museum** is a three-story, adobe, water-powered flour mill built at the end of the nineteenth century that has been turned into a local history museum. The mill's original equipment is intact but is used only for demonstration. Additionally, the mill contains photos, documents, and exhibits about its history. Though it is usually open weekends, it's best to check in advance. The mill offers an annual Labor Day Millfest.

It's located two miles north of Mora on Hwy 518. Turn right at the Cleveland Roller Mill sign.
Cleveland, NM 87715
(575) 387-2645
http://www.clevelandrollermillmuseum.org/

COLFAX AND COLD BEER

Colfax was once a bustling town, but it is no more. However, people do like to drink, and so while the town disappeared, there is still a tavern. The **Colfax Tavern and Grill** is, as they like to say, located in Cold Beer, New Mexico. And the sign certainly proclaims that.

In reality, it sits in the middle of nowhere on US 64 about 13 miles past Cimarron at the junction with NM 505. It's one of those places you can't miss because there's nothing else around to distract you. If you see a building around there, especially if it has a sign that says Cold Beer, it's probably the Colfax Tavern.
(575) 376-2229
https://www.facebook.com/ColdBeerNM

CUERVO

Cuervo was founded in the very early 1900s as part of the Southern Pacific Railroad and subsequently became a cattle town. Between the railroad, cattle, and Route 66, Cuervo had churches, schools, and businesses. Today I-40 bisects the town but with no convenient exit. Without easy access Cuervo has become one of those bypassed towns. Ruins of shops and shells of homes stretch along the empty road. You'll find it along the frontage road of I-40, getting off at exit 291. There are ghostly buildings on both sides of I-40, but the southern side has more relics of that almost gone town.

EAGLE NEST

An Old West town on the Enchanted Circle, Eagle Nest offers lovely views, but like several of the towns along the route, winter is the big tourist season. The area offers just about every outdoor experience you can do in the snow. Eagle Nest does cater to summer visitors as well with gift shops and several restaurants along its Main Street.

It also offers **Eagle Nest Lake**, a 2,400-acre lake that is about four miles long and one mile wide and is stocked with fish in the summer. Although you can definitely take boats out on the lake, boat rental opportunities are not plentiful

FOLSOM

There isn't much to see in Folsom, but this village of less than 100 people has a really fun website. It is the home of Folsom Man, named after the area in which arrow points and animal bones were found. The site dates back to 8000 or 9000 BC. There is nothing to see at the site itself.

The **Folsom Museum**, established in 1966 in the Doherty Mercantile building, contains a collection of local artifacts and sponsors several events each year. It is generally open seasonally. Check the website or call for current hours.
101 Main St.
Folsom, NM 88419
(575) 278-2122
http://www.folsomvillage.com/

FORT UNION (SEE ALSO LAS VEGAS)

Fort Union is about twenty-eight miles away from Las Vegas at I-25 and exit 366 (Watrous). It makes a fascinating historical side trip. It's also a great destination for photographers.

At one time, the land that is currently the state of New Mexico was part of Spanish Mexico—settled by Spanish colonists under land grants from the King of Spain. But after the Mexican-American War in 1846-47, the land of New Mexico became a United States territory and was protected by the US Army. At that point the protection was for settlers and commerce against Native Americans, who were less than pleased at the encroachment on their land. Fort Union was one of the forts constructed beginning in 1851.

Although the location was well-chosen, the construction was shoddy and the fort soon began to deteriorate. When the Civil War came, the fear that the Confederacy might invade New Mexico spurred the construction of the second fort, this one a star-shaped earthen fort. Hardly better constructed than the first Fort Union, little is left except scars on the plains.
The Battle of Glorieta Pass ended the Confederacy's drive into New Mexico and the use of that second fort. There was a third incarnation of Fort Union, the remains of which still fascinate today. This sprawling installation, started in 1863, became a major military post protecting settlers and trade. It contained warehouses, shops, a laundry, and a military prison.

It also offered something rare and important—a hospital with a surgeon, assistant surgeon, and other personnel. Open to soldiers and their families, it was one of the best medical facilities in the West. Civilians who paid a fee for the services could also use the medical facility.

The military campaigns effectively ended the threats from the Native American tribes. Fort Union was abandoned in 1891.

For years, Fort Union fell quietly into ruin—the adobe walls crumbled without maintenance, allowing rain, snow, and wind to erode the buildings. The private owners of the land wanted it for cattle grazing and had no interest in saving the fort's structures. But there were conservation groups fighting to save it, and eventually Fort Union National Monument was created in 1956. Efforts immediately began to stabilize the buildings. The visitor center opened in 1959.

Today, Fort Union is open to the public for special events, regular ranger-led walks, and self-guided exploration. A system of information stations explains the ruins and life in the fort. There is one stop that visitors should make on their way into or out of the fort. Pull over at the sign for information on the Santa Fe Trail and see the actual ruts and arroyos left by the wagons. Within the fort itself you can also find a hand-lettered sign pointing to some of the wagon ruts. http://www.nps.gov/foun/index.htm

GLENRIO

This Route 66 ghost town off I-40 is so far east that it just about slips over into Texas. Despite having a historic district listed on the National Register, there's not much left here—another casualty of shifting road and travel patterns. When I-40 bypassed the town, Glenrio effectively died.

GLORIETA

The area around Glorieta was the site of the 1862 Battle of Glorieta Pass, a battle that turned out to be the beginning of the end of Confederate ambitions to cut off the West from the Union.

Initially, the Confederate Army was successful. They marched along the Rio Grande, taking towns along the way, but their achievements impelled Colorado troops to move south into the fight. The two forces met at Glorieta Pass with a Confederate victory, but this one was a bit pyrrhic for the Confederates. The destruction of their supply wagons forced them to retreat down the river. More skirmishes followed, but the Confederates were still short of supplies. Outnumbered and inadequately provisioned, they kept retreating until eventually the troops retreated into Texas.

Visitors can walk the **Glorieta Battlefield Trail** (go to the Visitor Center first for access) or reserve a spot on a ranger-led van tour of the site. http://www.nps.gov/peco/index.htm

LAS VEGAS (SEE ALSO FORT UNION)

Drivers often notice something unusual in the Northeast part of the state—New Mexico has its own Las Vegas, but ours is much older. New Mexico's Las Vegas is a colonial city, established on a land grant in 1835. It was originally laid out in the traditional style, with a central plaza surrounded by buildings. That historic plaza still exists, and strolling around the tree-shaded square is still a popular pastime. Fans of the television series Longmire may recognize the plaza in background shots of the town.

Las Vegas was a commercial powerhouse in the early years. It was a major stop on the Santa Fe Trail, which brought goods from Missouri into Santa Fe. Stagecoaches stopped in Las Vegas, and so did cattle in the 1867 and 1868 Goodnight-Loving trail cattle drives. That name came from two cattlemen—Charles Goodnight and Oliver Loving—who saw the potential beef market for settlers and soldiers stationed at Army forts in New Mexico, including Fort Sumner (See Fort Sumner, and Loving).

When the railroad arrived, Las Vegas continued to thrive. The town became a regional hub, and new settlers poured in, sparking a grand pastiche of building styles. Las Vegas became one of the largest cities in the American Southwest.

The town was prosperous, but it was not tame; it attracted outlaws as well as merchants. This Wild West town has known Doc Holliday, who had his dental office here, and his girlfriend, Big Nose Kate, as well as Jesse James, Billy the Kid, Wyatt Earp, and more.

Its diverse history created historic neighborhoods with hundreds of buildings on the National Register of Historic Places. **The Las Vegas Citizens Committee for Historic Preservation** offers a yearly tour with docents stationed to talk about the unique features of the most popular locations.

Visit their website to put together a DIY architectural tour (click on Walking Tours). Stop in at their office to learn more

about historic Las Vegas, but call ahead for the hours of operation.
116 Bridge St.
Las Vegas, NM 87701
(505) 425-8803
http://www.lvcchp.org/

Although the light of economic glory moved on, there is still much to see in Las Vegas, and anyone interested in historic architectural styles will surely fall in love with this town.

HISTORIC ARCHITECTURE AND RAILROAD HISTORY
The historic parts of the city are well worth a visit. There are stone buildings and a mix of Victorian architecture—Queen Anne, Romanesque, Italianate, and more.

There's one historic building that's doubly famous. The Carnegie Library was built in 1903 and is the only surviving Carnegie Library left in New Mexico. Industrialist and philanthropist Andrew Carnegie donated more than $40 million over two decades to build 1,679 libraries in communities across America, long before the public library system was created. The **Carnegie Library** in Las Vegas was built in the Neo-Classical Revival style and still operates as a library.
500 National Ave.
Las Vegas, NM 87701
(505) 426-3304; (505) 454-1403
http://www.lasvegasnm.gov/community/carnegie_library/index.php

Las Vegas is also home to one of the few remaining Harvey House hotels. For years the **Hotel Castenada** was a sad picture of neglect. After decades of slow deterioration, Arizona developer Allan Affeldt purchased the formerly gorgeous Mission Revival building in 2014 and is bringing it back to its former glory. There is no date yet as to when it will open for guests, but the Facebook page lists updates and special events.
https://www.facebook.com/CastanedaHotel/

Located next door is the renovated historic railroad station at Railroad Street and Lincoln Avenue. It now serves as a **Visitor Center** and a stop on Amtrak's Southwest Chief train, but the

93

hotel was there for guests traveling on the famed AT&SF trains.
500 Railroad Ave.
Las Vegas, NM 87701
(505) 425-3707
(800) 832-5947
http://www.visitlasvegasnm.com/

Affeldt is also upgrading another Las Vegas signature hotel, the historic **Plaza Hotel** on the plaza in downtown Las Vegas. Built in 1882, its Italianate architecture makes it a distinctively regal building.
230 Plaza
Las Vegas, NM 87701
(505) 425-3591
http://plazahotellvnm.com/

One further standout building is known today as **Montezuma Castle**. Technically located in the town of Montezuma, which is six miles from Las Vegas, it is currently home to United World College. It began as the Montezuma, a luxury Harvey House hotel/resort that boasted access to natural hot springs and offered guests billiards and even bowling. It was the first building in New Mexico to have electric lights and an elevator. The railroad even built a spur to take visitors to the Montezuma.

The current building is actually its third incarnation. It was destroyed by fire in 1884, rebuilt, and then partially rebuilt after another fire two years later.

The building is not open to the public except during tours generally offered Saturday afternoon during the school year. Check their website for the dates of upcoming tours http://www.uwc-United States.org/page.cfm?p=527 or call (505) 454-4221.

Although usually closed to visitors, there is, however, a corner of United World College campus that is open to visitors. **Dwan Light Sanctuary**, designed by Virginia Dwan, Charles Ross, and Laban Wingert, is a place of meditation. The stark circular structure is generally bare, save for 12 large prisms that spread light and rainbows across the floor and walls. There are no windows and no other light source.

For day trips, there's the **Las Vegas Wildlife Refuge**—well over 8,000 acres open for hiking, bird-watching, hunting, and special events. It's also a stop for Sandhill cranes who come through in the fall on their way south. If you're not into hiking, you can drive the eight-mile auto loop through the refuge. http://www.fws.gov/refuge/las_vegas/

RATON

There's a story behind just about every town in New Mexico, including Raton (pronounced rat-tone). The name comes from the word "ratoncito," which is Spanish for mouse. It is speculated that the town was named after the numerous chipmunks in the area.

The Raton area was of crucial importance on the Santa Fe Trail, but in the 1820s it was quite dangerous for wagons to use that route through the Sangre de Cristo Mountains. The Raton Pass was narrow, steep, and filled with rocks. Eventually, another shorter and less treacherous route, the Cimarron Route, was developed. The Raton branch of the trail eventually fell out of favor, allowing the town of Cimarron to boom.

But that wasn't the end of the Raton Pass. By the end of the Civil War, enterprising Richens Wootton, with labor provided by the Utes, graded and improved 27 miles of the most dangerous part of the Raton Pass, making it safer and more popular. It became a quite profitable toll road, but it's worth noting that Wootton never charged Native Americans to use the road. He eventually sold the land to the AT&SF Railroad.

Start your visit at the **Raton Museum**, but don't miss the other marvelous historic buildings.
108 S Second St.
Raton, NM 87740
(575) 445-8979
http://www.theratonmuseum.org/

Raton's Downtown Historic District is listed on the National Register of Historic Places and encompasses 95 historic buildings. Like all successful towns, Raton had theaters. Today, the **Shuler**, which opened in 1915, still welcomes theatergoers and visitors. Upgraded and renovated, the owners have maintained the building's original architecture and design. The Shuler still has three of the original drop curtains and eight WPA murals depicting the history of Raton and the surrounding area from the 1840s to the 1920s.

131 N Second St.
Raton, NM 87740
(575)445-4746
http://shulertheater.com/

A bit newer, the **El Raton** has been a movie theater since the 1930s and is open for movie viewing.

111 N Second St.
Raton, NM 87740
(575) 445-7008
http://www.elratontheatre.com/

Another historic destination is a must-visit, but this one is a shopping opportunity that you will find in very few other places. **Solano's Boot & Western Wear** is known for its selection of unique boots. But the store also has a very unusual collection; one they swear is the largest of its kind in the world. Their cowboy hat "cemetery" contains over three hundred real and really used cowboy hats, each labeled with the name of the donor. Next door is a leather-working shop that is pure Western and a delight to visit.

101 S Second St.
Raton, NM 87740
(575) 445-2632
https://www.solanoswesternwear.com

The 1910 **Wells Fargo Express Building**, in Spanish Mission Revival style, is home to the Raton Arts & Humanities Council and an art gallery.

145 S First St.
Raton, New Mexico, 87740
(575) 445–2052
http://www.ratonarts.org/

Outside the city, there's still more to see. Raton is the nearest city to the **Capulin Volcano National Monument**, a cinder cone volcano. You can take a drive up the paved road that spirals up to the rim and hike along the trails. Plan on bringing in your own food and water, and pay attention to the time of year you visit. The NPS website notes that the restrooms are closed from mid-October to mid-May.

The visitor center features exhibits about the volcano, the area's geology, natural and cultural history, and offers educational programs about volcanoes. There is also a video presentation about the volcano.
http://www.nps.gov/cavo/index.htm

The **NRA Whittington Center** caters to gun enthusiasts of all ages and genders across its 33,000 acres. The center offers a variety of courses, hunting experiences, and shooting ranges. There's also a variety of lodging options.
34025 US-64
Raton, NM 87740
http://www.nrawc.org/

SPECIAL FOCUS: VERMEJO PARK RANCH

The largest private landowner in New Mexico is Ted Turner. His Vermejo Park Ranch, near Raton, comes in at almost the size of Rhode Island. It would make a very respectable national park, but this magnificent acreage has been turned into a hunting and fishing lodge, with a serious outdoor exploration aspect. Guests can row across an alpine lake, watch cow elks and their calves, try some skeet shooting, and photograph bison and eagles, or horse ride through the high country. Not enough to do? With a guide you can hike through abandoned towns, learn about forest management, peer through binoculars at raptors, or learn about the geology of the land and efforts to bring back some of the Ranch's original species.

Private guest rooms are in the half dozen "cottages." Each of these stone architectural beauties has about four to six rooms with a comfortable ranch feel inside. Since Vermejo is focused on nature and unplugging from the world, you won't find phones or televisions in any of these rooms, and certainly not Wi-Fi

---

(although you can access Wi-Fi in the main lodge). Each cottage has a community living area with a phone (in case your cell phone doesn't work). The larger rooms welcome guests with stone fireplaces, comfy couches, and chairs.

The food is gourmet and the views off the veranda are as beautiful as the food is delicious.
http://www.vermejoparkranch.com/

SANTA ROSA (SEE ALSO FORT SUMNER)

Santa Rosa is noteworthy as a place to go SCUBA diving. Diving underwater in New Mexico strikes many as almost impossible, but Santa Rosa is home to an oddity known as the **Blue Hole**— an 80-foot-deep spring famous for its clear blue water. There's a diving school on the premises. By the way, the temperature is always a nicely chilled 61 degrees.
1085 Blue Hole Road
Santa Rosa, NM 88435
(575) 472-3763
 http://santarosabluehole.com/

Anyone on a Route 66-themed trip needs to visit the **Route 66 Auto Museum**. It was started by James Cordova as place for his vintage car collection and has grown to include not only beautifully restored vehicles but memorabilia from that era.
2411 Historic Route 66
Santa Rosa, NM 88435
(575) 472-1966

SPRINGER

Colfax County Courthouse, listed on the National Register of Historic Places, was not only the seat of Colfax County government from 1881 to 1897, it was also the site of one of the last shoot-outs of the Colfax County War, which took place on its front lawn. Today, it houses a museum on the Santa Fe Trail.
614 Maxwell Ave.
Springer, NM 87747

SPECIAL FOCUS: MAXWELL LAND GRANT

Much of the land through this part of New Mexico was once part of the Maxwell Land Grant, and that story starts with a man from Taos called Charles Beaubien. He was a French Canadian who came to New Mexico in 1823 and became a wealthy merchant. But he wanted to own land, a lot of land. So he teamed up with Guadalupe Miranda, private secretary to Governor Manuel Armijo, to speed up the process of acquiring acreage.

It probably surprised no one that not only did they get the land, but they immediately deeded almost a quarter back to the governor. Another quarter went to Charles Bent, who was later appointed governor of the territory of New Mexico.

The people of the Taos Pueblo were not quite as pleased with the arrangement as the new landowners—the grant included their traditional grazing land. After a few years of going back and forth between incoming governors who alternatively upheld and negated the grant, the land grab was finally upheld.

In the meantime, Beaubien wanted to enlarge his holdings even further and turned to his son-in-law Lucien Maxwell to help him. Through a series of purchases in 1864 and 1867, Maxwell kept growing the land given in the original grant. When Beaubien died, Maxwell bought all the shares held by the heirs, and then he bought the land shares held by the heirs of Charles Bent.

By 1869, the Maxwell land grant under Lucien Maxwell's sole ownership included nearly two million acres extending from south of Cimarron into southern Colorado, making him the single largest land owner in the United States.

For years, Maxwell appeared to be a benign landowner. Settlers could pay their rent in produce, and he leased claims to miners to work their stakes. But in 1870 he decided to sell off most of his land to investors. That's when things soured. Eventually the newest owners wanted to claim the total grant of two million acres, but the government decided that a single grant couldn't be anywhere near that large, and that all but 97,000 acres were public domain. That still left quite a bit of land privately held. No one was happy with that decision. It didn't satisfy the investors, or the small farmers and miners felt they had the right

Russell's Truck and Travel Museum Gallery isn't quite as strange a combination as it seems. The Russell family, who own several truck stops in New Mexico, have a passion for cars. What better place to keep them than at a truck stop/60s-style diner along one of New Mexico's interstates? You'll find it at the Springer exit off I-25. Stop in—the food is good and the cars are even better.

TUCUMCARI

Depending on the direction of your travel, Tucumcari is either the first city you'll see along I-40 going west into New Mexico, or the last place you'll see going east to leave.

It's often said that the name is Comanche in origin, derived from tukamukaru, which is said to mean "to lie in wait for something or someone." Others say it means "lookout point." In short, no one really knows. But, regardless of the origin of its name, Tucumcari started as a railroad town that survived because of its place on Route 66. Even today, the nostalgia factor is prominent around town. Much of the original Route 66 attractions and neon remain. In addition, Tucumcari offers a wonderful collection of wall murals by Doug and Sharon Quarles depicting its history.

The living nostalgia highlights include the somewhat politically incorrect but much loved **Tee Pee Curios** with its large teepee entrance.
924 E Route 66
Tucumari, NM 88401
(575) 461-3773
https://www.facebook.com/teepeecurios/

The **Blue Swallow Motel** has been welcoming travelers along Route 66 with its cheery neon sign since it opened in 1940. The rooms have all the modern conveniences but in mid-century style and décor.
815 E Route 66
Tucumcari, NM 88401
(575) 461-9849
http://blueswallowmotel.com/

The **Tucumcari Train Depot** is a restored 1926 Spanish mission-style historic railroad depot that is in the process of becoming a railroad museum.
103 West Railroad Ave.
Tucumcari, NM 88401
(575) 461-4273

Opened in 1939, the Art Deco **Odeon Theater** is still delighting audiences, one movie at a time. The building, on the National Register for Historic Places, is a one-screen theater seating around 700 moviegoers. There is no website.
123 S Second St.
Tucumcari, NM 88401
(575) 461-0100

Don't be surprised to see folks with cameras posing by the **Tucumcari Convention Center**. Route 66 fans stop here to snap photos of its Route 66 Monument and enjoy the New Mexico Route 66 Museum.

The base of the sculpture by Tom Coffin is a tire, road, and tread motif, on a pyramid with a larger than life chrome tailfin. The taillights light up at night.
1500 W Route 66
Tucumcari, NM 88401

Another reason you'll find people pulling into the parking lot, this time going around the back, is for the **New Mexico Route 66 Museum**. Route 66 nostalgia and memorabilia find a home in this new museum. http://www.nmrt66museum.org/

Although Tucumcari is famous for its Route 66 history, the area was home to residents as far back as the Triassic Period around 153 to 148 million years ago, when dinosaurs roamed the land. **Mesalands Community College Dinosaur Museum** houses replicas and original fossils ranging from small footprint casts to the forty-foot-long skeleton of Torvosaurus, a rare carnivore relative of Tyrannosaurus rex. Interesting side note: the bronze castings were made at the school's own foundry. In fact, every spring the college offers an Iron Pour Workshop, but there are also opportunities to observe the pouring process and participate in special activities for the community as well.
222 E Laughlin St.
Tucumcari, NM 88401
(575) 461-3466
http://www.mesalands.edu/community/dinosaur-museum/

WATROUS (SEE FORT UNION)

The key attraction is Fort Union, and that is definitely worth a visit.

CENTRAL

This region is dominated by New Mexico's largest city, Albuquerque, but there's much to discover.

ALBUQUERQUE (SEE ALSO SANDIA PARK AND CORRALES)

By far the largest city in New Mexico, Albuquerque city proper is home to over 500,000 residents, but the greater metro area includes about one million people in a state of just over two million.

The city was officially founded in 1706 when King Philip of Spain established a new villa (city) on the banks of the Rio Grande. The new colony was named after the Duke of Alburquerque (note the additional "r") to be called La Villa de Alburquerque in his honor. Over the centuries the first "r" was dropped, leaving the modern spelling "Albuquerque." The city's nickname ultimately became Duke City, although when residents are feeling playful, it's called Albuquirky. Other times the long name is shorted to ABQ.

In 1846, control of the territory that includes Albuquerque shifted from Mexico to the United States. But the area truly came into its own through advances in transportation. On April 10, 1880, the tracks of the Atchison Topeka & Santa Fe reached Albuquerque, and it transformed the town into a major city.

As with every other place the railroad blessed with its technology, stores and saloons sprouted, eventually creating a commercial district known as New Town. The original Albuquerque came to be called Old Town. Of course they both grew into one another, but even today, Albuquerque prizes it picturesque Old Town.

Albuquerque is situated along the banks of the Rio Grande. Although in the past periodic and unpredictable flooding could devastate the city, today the river has been tamed and the result is a recreational area beloved by residents.

CIBOLA NATIONAL FOREST AND THE CREST
Albuquerque also abuts the Cibola National Forest, providing miles of hiking and acres of room for outdoor activities. One popular destination is Sandia Crest. Everyone knows about the **Sandia Peak Tramway**. It is billed as 2.7 miles from bottom to top—4,000 feet in about 15 minutes. It is quite a spectacular ride, and its view is incredible too. http://sandiapeak.com/index.php?page=sandia-peak-tramway

As wonderful as the ride is (and as gorgeous the view), there's another way to go up even higher, reaching the very top of the Crest. To get there, take Route 14 north (also called the Turquoise Trail), and turn onto NM 536 north. It's a gorgeous, hairpin drive right through the Cibola National Forest. It's worth the time to get there.

The Crest offers a jaw-dropping view of the city. Under the right conditions, hang gliders use the updrafts to ride the wind. There are walking trails into the forest that offer peekaboo views and a walkway along the peak. Even if you're acclimated to Albuquerque's mile-high altitude, the crest at 10,679 feet can leave you breathless—walk slowly and pause often.

While you're at the Crest marveling at the views of the city, you can also see the **Antenna Farm**. The area is filled with RF (radio frequency) towers used in telecommunications. It's not possible to enter the area and get up close with the towers for safety reasons, but even outside the fence, it's an impressive sight.

The tram is located in Albuquerque, but the crest itself is actually in a mountain hamlet called Sandia Park.

OPEN SPACE
In addition to the extensive acreage provided by the national forest, Albuquerque itself has designated whole swaths of land as part of the Open Space program, creating everything from horse trails to birdwatching opportunities as well as water-based recreation.

The **Rio Grande Valley State Park** hugs the Rio Grande River on one side and offers birding blinds on the other, with the spectacular Sandia Mountains as the backdrop.
https://www.cabq.gov/parksandrecreation/open-space/lands/rio-grande-valley-state-park

Another beautiful spot is **Elena Gallegos Open Space**, which backs onto the Cibola National Forest.
https://www.cabq.gov/parksandrecreation/open-space/lands/elena-gallegos-open-space

The **Open Space Visitor Center** located along the Rio Grande offers special programs and events.
6500 Coors Blvd. NW
Albuquerque, NM 87120
(505) 897-8831
https://www.cabq.gov/parksandrecreation/open-space/open-space-visitor-center

SPECIAL FOCUS: PUEBLO MONTANO PARK AND THE WOOD CARVINGS OF MARK CHAVEZ

In 2003, a fire devastated the Bosque (the woods along the Rio Grande) and Pueblo Montano Park, destroying trees and vegetation. Rather than uprooting the dead trees, the park has been turned into an unusual sculptural garden through the chainsaw artistry of Mark Chavez.

Chavez was one of the firefighters who fought the Bosque blaze. Now retired to pursue his love of wood carving, Chavez took the charred hulks and made them into owls, turtles, birds, and a beautiful eagle with spread wings. There's also a firefighter with his foot on a vanquished dragon in honor of the men and women who quelled the blaze.

"You take this big, barren chunk of wood that doesn't look like it's good for anything except maybe to cut up and burn for firewood, and you start chiseling away at it, and, little by little, something starts forming. And in the end, something beautiful is made out of something that other people might see as worthless. I feel like our lives are shaped that way," said Chavez when the project was first announced.

Albuquerque is a city where history, art, and nature form a
variegated tapestry of opportunities for visitors. The hills
around the city provide the ingredients for burgeoning
distilleries. There is prehistoric wall art (think petroglyphs)
and much newer murals by our street artists. You can even try
your hand at creating your own art. The city's diverse history
has made it a laboratory for architectural innovation. Our
museums showcase the gifts of nature and our rich history.

RAILROAD HISTORY
The coming of the railroad in 1880 quite literally made the city
of Albuquerque, creating a whole new section along Central
Avenue. The railroad had a vast complex built to service the
trains and manage the railroad system. Manufacturing and
shipping businesses took advantage of the easy rail
connections. The long-gone Alvarado Hotel attracted travelers
who flocked to see the Southwest via the Atchison Topeka &
Santa Fe. It became famous for the pottery and jewelry in its
Indian Building. Visitors could even watch the artisans at
work.

The railroad became the largest employer in town, creating a
financial windfall and an architectural playground as the
newcomers wanted their homes to reflect their Midwest roots.
The area still shelters some of these early homes, and
Downtown Albuquerque is studded with some of the early
buildings dating back to the rise of the railroad.

The biggest and perhaps most beloved architectural relic is the
Rail Yards, which is a wildly popular photographic ruin and a
quirky event centerpiece. Built between 1914 and 1924, it
serviced the trains that brought goods and people to the
Southwest and further.

As the importance of the railroad faded, so did the **Rail Yards**, but it never lost its allure for the people of Albuquerque who regularly snuck in to stare at the vast cathedral-like spaces, and poke cameras through broken windows. Today, the city has cleaned up the blacksmith shop and it now hosts the Rail Yards Market on Sundays (spring through fall) as well as other special events. The Yards have also served as a movie set for several films, including one of the Terminators.
777 First St. SW
Albuquerque, NM 87102
https://www.facebook.com/RailYardsMarket

Also on the grounds is the **Wheels Museum**, but the hours are very limited. Call (505) 243-6269 for information.
http://wheelsmuseum.org/

Visitors can also watch a piece of railroad history being restored as the New Mexico Steam Locomotive and Railroad Historical Society volunteers work on a **Baldwin 4-8-4 Steam Locomotive, AT&SF No. 2926**. Their goal is to bring the historic engine to operational status, but the target date is a bit elusive. Volunteers are always welcome, but so are interested visitors.
1833 Eighth St. NW (I-40, south of the interstate)
Albuquerque, NM 87102
(505) 246-2926
http://www.nmslrhs.org/

ROUTE 66 HISTORY
After the railroad lost its importance, the automobile took its place as a driving economic force. Route 66 went right through the center of the city along the section of town made commercially successful by the railroad.

Although today it is Central Avenue that is famous as the old Route 66 (with signs proclaiming its heritage), for a time, Fourth Street was the designated historic road. From 1926 through 1937, drivers heading to California from Chicago would take a cutoff near Santa Rosa and head north to Santa Fe. Then they would follow the road back south to Albuquerque along Fourth Street.

The result is that something quirky happens at the corner of Central and Fourth—it's where **Route 66 and Route 66 meet**. A large sign proudly announces this unusual confluence. After 1937, Central Avenue became and remained the Mother Road. Visitors can still see some of the old motels that once beckon tired drivers.

Maisel's Indian Trading Post is one of the original Route 66 landmark businesses. A visit to Maisel's in Downtown is a great shopping opportunity, but the notable murals gracing the walls and its architecture (it's a John Gaw Meem building done in Pueblo Revival style) have given it a serious dose of historic gravitas.
510 Central Ave. SW
Albuquerque, NM 87102
(505) 242-6526
http://skipmaisels.com/

The **Route 66 Diner** doesn't date back that far, but it celebrates the 1950s and the Route 66 spirit. And it's a favorite with locals and tourists.
1405 Central Ave. NE
Albuquerque, NM 87106
(505) 247-1421
http://www.66diner.com/index.html

Once a year in July, the Nob Hill neighborhood has their Route 66 Festival with historic automobiles, live music, and great strolling.

SPECIAL FOCUS: ROUTE 66

The mass production of the automobile eventually changed just about everything in this country, from the way goods were shipped to the way people vacationed. It certainly changed the highway system. What good is a car if you can't go anywhere? Dirt roads became paved, and a system of interconnected routes invited exploration and travel.

Although several other highways were developed around the same time, Route 66 caught the imagination and inflamed America's passion to travel as no other.

Route 66 began in 1926 when the first federal highway system was launched, but what drivers found was nothing like the highways of today. In fact, Route 66 was "created" by putting up Route 66 signs on roads that had already been built by local, state, and the federal government.

The resulting patchwork roadway could be "moved" by simply removing the signs from one road and placing them on another. This meant that there were different versions of Route 66. These new alignments could make a town or a business boom or go bust.

The Route often ran right through the center of a town, giving it the nickname of America's Main Street. When John Steinbeck wrote The Grapes of Wrath, it picked up another nickname—The Mother Road, the road of flight when about a quarter million people used it to flee the devastating drought of the 1930s.

Not only was Route 66 a quilt of small roads, it was a quilt of often unpaved or poorly paved roads. In the 1930s, the government decided to regulate the quality of the roads that would be included in the highway system. By 1938 it was a continuously paved road —all 2,400 miles.

All those cars and all those people needed services. Motels (motor hotels), gas stations, and restaurants sprung up. Competition drove innovation in eye-catching designs and logos. Neon lit the night. Motels masqueraded as teepees. A blue whale heralded a swimming hole. Many of these are still preserved today and are visited by millions taking Route 66-themed journeys.

Over time fast, efficient interstates replaced the old roads. In 1985 the government officially decommissioned Route 66. But the Mother Road, the Main Street of America, lived on. Driving that mish-mashed system was more fun than speeding from state to state. Americans, and visitors from outside the country, began to take to Route 66 once again. Today, there's no shortage of books, articles, and websites helping travelers plan their drive back into history.

This is a city of neighborhoods, quilted together to form something that exceeds their sum.

Note: The city is divided into quadrants with Central Avenue dividing the city between north and south. But in terms of addresses and locations, it can mean that places on the north side of the street are technically in a different quadrant of the city, even though it's just across the street from an address on the south side of the city. This is particularly true in Nob Hill and Downtown.

Old Town

Old Town is the historic heart of the city and the best place to feel its roots. On the north side of the plaza is the **San Felipe de Neri Church.** The original building was constructed in 1706, but it collapsed after an unusually heavy rain in 1792. The church that now stands on the Old Town Plaza was built in 1793 and is the oldest building in the city.

It is still active, and visitors can stop by anytime the church is open. The church and the setting are quite beautiful and are often photographed.
2005 N Plaza St. NW
Albuquerque, NM 87104
(505) 243-4628
http://sanfelipedeneri.org/

Located in historic Old Town is the rather quirky **Rattlesnake Museum**.
202 San Felipe St. NW
Albuquerque, NM 87104
(505) 242-6569
http://www.rattlesnakes.com

Did You Know...

A Beloved Cartoon Character Is Also Our State Bird?

The roadrunner is found throughout the state and is a form of ground cuckoo. Although generally flightless, it can run up to twenty miles per hour and can run down prey. Roadrunners eat small animals like mice and lizards, insects, and even small birds. The Road Runner was part of a cartoon pair (along with Wile E. Coyote), but the real thing looks and acts very differently from the cartoon version.

There's plenty of galleries and shopping in Old Town along the main streets and tucked into plazas. Strolling through the area is a favored pastime.

If photographic art is your passion, the **Albuquerque Photographers Gallery** should be a stop on your stroll through the area. The gallery hosts the work of some of the best artists in the city.
303 Romero St. NW
Albuquerque, NM 87104
(505 244-9195
http://www.abqphotographersgallery.com

Note: Although street parking can be hard to find, parking lots border the area, including one next to the Albuquerque Museum of Art and History with plenty of spaces and easy access for a reasonable fee.

Nob Hill
Situated along historic Route 66 on Central Avenue, Nob Hill once boasted the businesses and signs that drew in drivers. Motor lodges, restaurants, and automobile-based businesses lined the road. Most are gone, but Nob Hill has reinvented itself into an upscale shopping area. There are still restaurants galore, but the shops are now filled with home décor items, clothing, and gourmet food.

There are two stellar places in Nob Hill to shop for sleek modern yet Southwest-style jewelry—Lilly Barrack and Gertrude Zachery. Both stores have other locations in Albuquerque but not as conveniently located, almost across from each other in Nob Hill. Sisters Barrack and Zachery spent many years in gentle competition until Zachery's death in 2013. The galleries have very different price points and different approaches to the design of jewelry. Both are gorgeous.

Lilly Barrack Jewelry & Gifts
3205 Central Ave. NE # 104,
Albuquerque, NM 87106
(505) 265-4147
http://www.lillybarrack.com/

Gertrude Zachary Jewelry
3300 Central Ave. SE
Albuquerque, NM 87106
(505) 766-4700
http://gertrudezachary.com/

Nob Hill is also home to the city's only art film movie theater, **The Guild.**
3405 Central Ave. NE
Albuquerque, NM 87106
(505) 255-1848
http://www.guildcinema.com/

University Area
All things appealing to students can be found along Central Avenue in the University area. And quite a lot of it appeals to visitors as well—especially those looking for well-priced restaurants, cafes, and funky shopping.

The city's beloved **Frontier Restaurant** has faced the main entrance of UNM since 1971. Although not part of the Route 66 or railroad history, it's open daily until 1:00 a.m. and serves good food at good prices in a place with almost no atmosphere, but surprisingly interesting art. Add a star if you like John Wayne.
2400 Central Ave. SE
Albuquerque, NM 87106
(505)266-0550
http://frontierrestaurant.com

Downtown
Originally the hub of the railroad, today Downtown is the center of business for the city. Honoring the now razed, but once-upon-a-time gorgeous Alvarado Hotel, the Mission Revival-style Alvarado Transportation Center is the hub for all regional transportation.

Downtown is the place for movies, restaurants, bars, art galleries (a personal favorite is Sumner & Dene), and some unusual shops—including Man's Hat Shop selling hats for 68+ years.

Sumner & Dene
517 Central Ave. NW
Albuquerque, NM 87102
(505)842-1400
http://www.sumnerdene.com

Man's Hat Shop
511 Central Ave. NW
Albuquerque, NM 87102
(505)247-9605
http://www.manshatshop.com

Jewelry and Native American arts shoppers will definitely
want to stop at **Skip Maisel**'s store, which boasts great old
Route 66 murals.
510 Central Ave. SW
Albuquerque, NM 87102
(505) 242-6526
http://skipmaisels.com

The Newest Zone
Like any city, Albuquerque has its more industrialized areas.
One of these is the birthplace of the city's fledgling craft spirits
upsurge and the innovative shipping container community
called Green Jeans Farmery. The area is located in the
northeast just north of I-40 and east of I-25 (the intersection
that we call the Big I).

Left Turn is Albuquerque's first and oldest distillery, opening
in November 2013. Their Old Tom-style gin, recalling the
eighteenth-century London version, is garnering awards on
both the national and worldwide level. Distiller Brian
Langwell also makes a rum flavored with macerated pinons—
definitely a shot of New Mexico in a glass. Their Blue Corn
Whiskey is another unique New Mexican flavor. They're open
for tours, tastings, and after-work cocktails.
2924 Girard Blvd. NE
Albuquerque, NM 87107
(505) 508-0508
https://www.facebook.com/LeftTurnDistilling/

Distillery365 opened in May 2015 as a brewery that is also a
distillery. Their spirits are named after New Mexico hiking
trails. In addition to Horsethief, their molasses-based rum, and

113

Holy Ghost New Mexico corn-based vodka (named after the New Mexico Holy Ghost trail), there's a Tres Pistolas (Three Gun) bourbon, all made from New Mexico ingredients. Stop by for one of their artisan beers or their spirited drinks. They also offer tours. Reservations are requested.
2921 Stanford Drive NE
Albuquerque, NM 87107
(505) 221-6281
http://distillery365.com

Green Jeans Farmery is a commercial plaza constructed entirely of shipping containers. It's the quirky vision of developer Roy Solomon, who seeks to create a new kind of community space of restaurants, breweries, and shops. Entranced with the possibilities of these containers, Solomon promises more to come, including, perhaps, a hydroponic garden.
3600 Cutler Ave. NE
Albuquerque, NM 87110
http://www.greenjeansfarmery.com

FROM STREET ART TO ANCIENT ART TO ARCHITECTURAL ART
Although there's plenty of conventional art throughout the city, Albuquerque has also embraced the far less conventional street art. Almost all has been done with the often enthusiastic permission of the building owners, and there are truly some spectacular murals.

One of the moving forces behind Albuquerque's unorthodox art is 516 Arts located on Central Avenue. Focused on showcasing traditional and contemporary work, the gallery mounted a special Street Art show/event/festival in 2010. The alley behind the gallery and the wall outside host some of the art from that event.

The LA Underground at 2000 Central Ave. SE supports street art (and aerosol painters) and almost always has some great graffiti on their wall.

The alley behind the Lobo Men's Shop at 2120 Central Ave. SE has gorgeous and meticulously executed aerosol wall art.

The walls of the arroyo by Acme Metals at 6142 Second St. NW host a long series of graffiti painted with permission as part of an aerosol festival held several years ago. Artists came from across the country and created what could be one of the longest graffiti-covered walls in the country.

The building that is tucked in between 3903 and 3907 Central Ave. NE sports an unusual wall mural. Painted by Joseph Sullivan, it actually turns the corner of the building.

Ancient Art: The Petroglyphs of Petroglyph National Monument
People have lived in New Mexico for centuries, and some of the earliest signs are the mysterious carvings known as petroglyphs. Albuquerque is home to Petroglyph National Monument located on the west side of the city.

There's a range of trails through the area, from the short and handicapped accessible to mile-long hikes through the mountains of dark rock.

Make your first stop the Visitor Center. There are no petroglyphs at that location, but you should pick up a map and information on the diversity of the trails and how to find the ones that will be the best for you to hike. You will need to drive to all the trail locations. Parking lots close at 5:00 p.m.
Petroglyph National Monument Visitor Center
Unser Blvd. at Western Trail

The park service provides these coordinates to help visitors find the Visitor Center on their GPS: Latitude: 35.139 Longitude: -106.711
(505) 899-0205
http://www.nps.gov/petr/

This video by the National Park Service is a great introduction to these intriguing markings. https://youtu.be/tj4haNMitUQ

Architectural Art
The **KiMo Theatre,** built in 1927, is one of the finest examples of the architectural style known as Pueblo Deco. It has been carefully restored and opened to the public for self-guided tours and for special performances.
423 Central Ave. NW
Albuquerque, NM 87102
(505) 768-3544
http://www.cabq.gov/culturalservices/kimo/kimo/about-the-theatre

There's also a sense of whimsy in the architecture of New Mexico, best expressed by Albuquerque-based **Bart Prince**, whose designs favor architecture as sculpture. A Bart Prince-designed house (privately owned) can be viewed from the outside at 3501 Monte Vista Blvd. NE. Another example of his unique style can be found at Casa de Suenos—a B&B located at the edge of Old Town at 310 Rio Grande Blvd. SW. Prince designed an entranceway in 1976 that added a futuristic touch to 1930s adobe-style complex. A bit incongruous, but fascinating.

Hands-On Art
Despite a wealth of art in the city, it's not easy to find opportunities for art workshops. The Albuquerque Visitors Bureau offers a great roundup of the events in town. Although there is no separate listing, type "art workshops" into the search box for a listing of hands-on events.
http://www.visitalbuquerque.org/abq365/events/

There's also an excellent art printmaking gallery/school/space in Albuquerque. **New Grounds Print Workshop and Gallery** offers day-long workshops on printmaking techniques (as well as several day workshops), but if nothing matches your schedule, they'll set up private instruction for any of their printmaking techniques.
3812 Central Ave. SE
Albuquerque, NM 87108
(505) 268-8952
http://www.newgroundsprintshop.com

ALBUQUERQUE'S MUSEUMS
From telephones to turquoise, Albuquerque offers a wild profusion of museums. Although many can be categorized into art, or history, or science, other collections defy easy classification and are uniquely Albuquerque.

This is a family-friendly city and the **BioPark** is definitely a highlight. Spread along the Rio Grande, and across the city, the BioPark is home to several attractions, all linked together by a pint-size special excursion train. The narrow-gauge Rio Line runs between the zoo, the aquarium and botanic garden, with Tingley Beach at the center. It's a fun way to see the BioPark and reach everything without having to move your car.

There's usually a new baby making an appearance somewhere at the Rio Grande Zoo, along with special shows and feedings, a beautiful aviary, and more. The Aquarium is another stop on the tiny railroad (or you can reach it separately by car), and when you've finished exploring the exhibits, walk behind it to the Botanic Gardens, with its Children's Fantasy Garden and a model railroad chugging through a tiny town. There's also the Heritage Farm representing farm life in Albuquerque in the 1920s and '30s. Of course, the gardens are magnificent. Don't miss the Japanese Garden.

Tingley Beach has the Bosque on one side and three fishing ponds on the other. You can rent a pedal boat, go fishing, or walk along the Bosque trails.
 903 10th St. SW
Albuquerque, NM 87102
(505) 768-2000
http://www.cabq.gov/culturalservices/biopark
https://www.cabq.gov/culturalservices/biopark/zoo
http://www.cabq.gov/culturalservices/biopark/garden
http://www.cabq.gov/culturalservices/biopark/aquarium
http://www.cabq.gov/culturalservices/biopark/tingley

Northeast

Albuquerque is a hot air ballooning capital, largely due to the famed Albuquerque Box, an early morning wind pattern that is prevalent in the fall. The winds blow from the north at lower elevations but from the south at higher elevations. Balloonists use these winds to take off in and around Balloon Fiesta Park, and fly the box back to their starting point.

The **Anderson-Abruzzo Albuquerque International Balloon Museum** is named after two of the record-setting balloonists. On August 11, 1978 Ben Abruzzo, Maxie Anderson, and Larry Newman took off from Presque Isle, Maine and made the first successful transatlantic hot air balloon crossing, landing in Miserey, France six days later.

Even without the backstory, the museum is quite fascinating with exhibits on the history and science of ballooning, a replica gondola available for photos, interactive exhibits, and numerous special artifacts. It's perfect for families, and intriguing for everyone.
9201 Balloon Museum Drive NE
Albuquerque NM 87113
(505) 768-7620
http://www.balloonmuseum.com/

Experience a bit of Albuquerque's beloved Balloon Fiesta here:
https://youtu.be/yczm2S5mESE

Northwest

On the border of Old Town, the city's museums conveniently line up for easy exploration. **The New Mexico Museum of**

Natural History & Science not only offers planetarium shows and 3-D movies, but also exhibits on science and natural history you'd expect in a museum with that title. Plus, it is now home to the first ever baby Pentaceratops skull. The rhinoceros-like, plant-eating dinosaur lived in northwest New Mexico around 73 to 76 million years ago when the climate was very different.

The museum is also home to an entire hall devoted to the history of the computer revolution. StartUp highlights the important Albuquerque connection.
1801 Mountain Road NW
Albuquerque, NM 87104
(505) 841-2800
http://nmnaturalhistory.org/

Albuquerque Museum of Art and History offers an innovative blending of art and history plus intriguing special exhibits and lectures. The museum was designed by internationally known Albuquerque architect Antoine Predock in 1979, and expanded in 2005.

The museum's ongoing exhibit called Only in Albuquerque focuses on the unique and intriguing history of the city. There's also over 60 pieces of sculpture, including several intriguing large pieces that greet visitors. Regular docent-led tours of the sculptures and the exhibits are available.
2000 Mountain Road NW
Albuquerque, NM 87104
(505) 242-4600
http://albuquerquemuseum.org/

A winner for adults and children who love science is the hands-on science center **Explora!** One of the finest in the country, it encourages the love and learning of science, technology, and art with innovative activities at specially constructed child-size tables filled with interactive experiences. On Fridays every other month, they invite adults only (18 or older) to come and play.
1701 Mountain Road NW
Albuquerque, NM 87104
(505) 224-8300
http://www.explora.us/en/

119

Any or all make a great day destination, and there are plenty of places to eat and shops to explore in Old Town (just behind the Albuquerque Museum of Art and History).

Everyone has their own view of history, and the Native American pueblos not only provide their personal perspective at the **Indian Pueblo Cultural Center**, but cultural performances, exhibits, and a gift shop featuring some of the finest Native American art and artisan crafts in the city. Enjoy Native American fusion cuisine in their restaurant. Check out their website for special classes featuring arts with a Native American twist. In summer, they have live music on their patio.
2401 12th St. NW
Albuquerque, NM 87104
(505) 843-7270
http://indianpueblo.org

Housed in the original 1906 Telephone Central Office in Downtown, the unique **Telephone Museum** is a trip back to phones even before the rotary dial—when you picked up the earpiece and spoke into a tube, asking the operator to connect you to your party. You can also learn about the early phone system in Albuquerque, dating back to 1919.

Beyond telephones, there are early teletype machines and the Baudot code that used perforations of paper tape to indicate letters of the alphabet. Exhibits also highlight the transatlantic cable that could carry what was then considered to be an amazing 72 conversations at a time.

The Telephone Museum of New Mexico provides a whole different perspective on the wonders of communication. The volunteer docents are ready to explain the antique devices and provide background to the exhibits.
110 Fourth St. NW
Albuquerque, NM 87102
(505) 280-4893
http://www.museumsusa.org/museums/info/1158187

There is probably no family in the country who knows more about the many facets of turquoise than the members of the Lowry family. The **Turquoise Museum** is their personal and extensive collection from all over the world. At one time, you could wander in and a member of the Lowry family (and there was always a family member around) would stop and answer your questions.

With the increase in the number of people fascinated by this not-always-blue stone, the Turquoise Museum has gotten more formal. Today, they offer two guided tours with hands-on exhibits and a lapidary demonstration. It's located on the edge of Old Town.

It's worth a visit to learn more about the story of turquoise—the colors of the stone, how it's used in jewelry, where it is mined, and more. If you plan on buying turquoise jewelry in New Mexico (and you should plan on doing that), you'll need to know the right questions to ask. The Lowry family will provide answers to those questions and more.
2107 Central Ave. NW
Albuquerque, NM 87104
(505) 247-8650
http://www.turquoisemuseum.com

Southeast
The **National Museum of Nuclear Science and History** is a bit out of the way, but it is well worth a visit—fascinating history and atomic energy science (including atomic pop culture) inside, and aircraft and missiles outside.
601 Eubank Blvd. SE
Albuquerque, NM 87123
(505) 245-2137.
http://www.nuclearmuseum.org/

The flagship campus of the University of New Mexico system hosts its own collection of museums and galleries spanning several disciplines. Its **Meteorite Museum** houses its collection of meteorites. It is advisable to check their website for hours.
200 Yale Blvd. SE
Albuquerque, NM 87106
(505) 277-2747
http://meteorite.unm.edu/meteorites/meteorite-museum/

The **Tamarind Institute** is focused on Fine Art Lithography. It offers free tours on most first Fridays of the month. Call for more information or to make reservations.
2500 Central Ave. SE
Albuquerque, NM 87106
(505) 277-3901
http://tamarind.unm.edu/

Southwest
Located in Downtown, the small thoughtful **Holocaust & Intolerance Museum of New Mexico** focuses on instances of genocide throughout history across many different countries. Although the emphasis is on the Holocaust in Germany, the museum also provides information on lesser-known mass killings including the Armenian Genocide. Those who helped save the victims are also honored.
616 Central Ave. SW
Albuquerque, NM 87102
(505) 247.0606
http://www.nmholocaustmuseum.org/index.php

The **National Hispanic Cultural Center** is one of the gems of the city. The architecture is starkly beautiful and Mayan-inspired. Its **Torreón** (or tower) houses the largest concave fresco in North America.

New Mexico master fresco artist Frederico Vigil spent close to a decade on the project carefully depicting over 3,000 years of Hispanic history in the broadest sense. From Europe to Mesoamerica and into the American Southwest, Vigil illustrates the complexities and diversity of the Hispanic experience. The **Torreón** is open and free to the public, but call to verify times and hours. Don't miss this one.

The NHCC also mounts special exhibits and offers excellent shows and performances. There's food to be had there as well, including the pan-Latin restaurant M'Tucci's Cocina Grill and a fun snack center with sandwiches, Pop Fizz.
1701 Fourth St. SW
Albuquerque, NM 87102
(505) 246-2261
http://www.nationalhispaniccenter.org

FOR THE LOVE OF SPEED

Located in the village of Los Ranchos de Albuquerque, the **Unser Racing Museum** is a specialty museum highlighting the Unser family's long legacy in car racing, including the evolution in design and engineering. Members of the Unser family have won nine Indianapolis 500 Races, and the museum presents their very personal view of racing.

Although you'll see plenty of historic race cars, exhibits also include perspectives from the Unser family—how racing affected them and how they affected racing. It's equal parts drama and tragedy.

The racing dynasty started when Louis Unser moved from Indiana to Colorado Springs in the early 1900s. At the same time Pikes Peak was being developed, Louis's three boys were all caught up in the thrill of motor vehicles. Jerry eventually moved to Albuquerque and opened a garage on Route 66. His four sons, Jerry, Jr, Louis, Bobby, and Al became the Albuquerque Unsers, astonishing the car racing world with their prowess. The exhibit area called Jerry's Garage pays homage to the man who started it all. Definitely sit down and watch the videos for insight into three generations of the family, their tenacity, and their speed on the track.

The Unsers never seemed to meet a race they didn't like—dirt track, NASCAR, sports car, but it was Indy that was most important. There's a whole exhibit area on that aspect of the Unser racing family.

There's an area for children (that adults will enjoy as well) with touch screen activities that are visually engaging and thoughtfully designed. One, for example, is a virtual pit and you can look down at the crew in action. Another gets into the physics of racing.

1776 Montano Road NW
Los Ranchos, NM 87107
(505) 341-1776
http://www.unserracingmuseum.com

Located off of I-40 just west of Albuquerque, **Sandia Speedway** offers a full program of racing across a variety of tracks: half- and quarter-mile paved ovals, high-banked 3/8-mile dirt ovals, and 1.7-mile road courses. And if you want to learn to drive fast and safe, they have the Charlie Fegan Performance Driving School.

100 Speedway Park Blvd. SW
Albuquerque, NM 87121
(505) 352-8888
http://racesandia.com/

Tours of Albuquerque
The city offers several charming ways to explore its natural beauty, ghostly past, and rich diversity.

Hop on a specially constructed trolley for a fascinating and comprehensive tour of the city. See film sites, Route 66 sites, major spots of history, the museums, and street murals. **ABQ Trolley** tours give visitors a taste of all that the city has to offer and a sense of the layout and neighborhoods. Specialty tours are periodically available throughout the year.

800 Rio Grande Blvd. NW
Albuquerque, NM 87104
(505) 240-8000
http://www.abqtrolley.com

For a history of Old Town, **Tours of Old Town** offers guided tours of the city's past and its legends. They offer a special ghost tour which is particularly fascinating and quite fun.

303 Romero St. NW (Plaza Don Luis - N120)
Albuquerque, NM 87104
(505) 246-TOUR (8687)
http://www.toursofoldtown.com

Once upon a time the Rio Grande was a mighty river that overflowed its banks and flooded parts of Albuquerque. Today it's been tamed, especially through the Albuquerque metro area, making for one sweet kayak trip. Paddle a bit, float a bit, avoid the sandbars, and enjoy the spectacular scenery. **Quiet Waters Paddling Adventures** generally offers tours from mid-March to mid-November (depending on weather and water conditions).

105 D Pleasant View Drive
Bernalillo, NM 87004
(505) 771-1234
(877) 45-FLOAT (877-453-5628)
http://www.quietwaterspaddling.com/

In addition to the companies offering tours, there's another way to explore New Mexico: through one-day enrichment trips and tours offered by **University of New Mexico at Albuquerque.** http://ce.unm.edu/enrichment/story-of-nm.php

Learn more about visiting Albuquerque and all the museums, events, and festivals by contacting Albuquerque Tourism: http://www.visitalbuquerque.org/

ALGODONES

Located between Santa Fe and Albuquerque, this hamlet is home to one of the new distilleries blooming in the deserts of New Mexico. Greg McAllister and P. David Pacheco are the forces behind the **Algodones Distillery**, and their gin is fragrant with lavender and juniper. The distillery also offers vodka, blue corn moonshine whiskey, and blue corn bourbon, all made with local botanicals and New Mexico blue corn. The Algodones Distillery has an onsite tasting room and tours given by appointment between 2:00 and 4:00 p.m. on Friday, Saturday, and Sunday. You must make arrangements through their website.
http://www.algodonesdistillery.com

BELEN

Belen, Spanish for Bethlehem, became a village in 1918, a town in 1940, and finally a city in 1966. Located about 30 minutes from Albuquerque, it is considered part of the Albuquerque Metropolitan Area.

Throughout the Southwest, when train travel was the best way to travel, the Harvey Houses became famous. The chain of hotels and train stations were largely built and run by Fred Harvey with the goal of enticing travelers to visit the romantic and exciting Southwest. (See Special Focus: Fred Harvey and His Magnificent Hotels.)

Little is left of that train-travel heritage, but in Belen, the **Harvey House Museum** is in the building that once housed one of the restaurants. The outside has been restored, and inside visitors will find a replica of a Harvey Girl bedroom
125

(they lived onsite), and memorabilia from that era. Call for hours.

The **Belen Model Railroad Club** is also quartered there and has a set of model trains open for visitors.
104 N First St.
Belen, NM 87002
(505) 861-0581
http://www.belen-nm.gov/Community/HarveyHouseBelen.htm

Ever wonder about how raw stone is quarried from the ground and turned into the beautiful facades that grace homes and buildings? Although the quarry itself is 20 miles west, the fabrication plant for **New Mexico Travertine** in Belen is where the rough, raw stone is sliced, cut, and polished. Visitors can rummage through their yard to find pieces of stone, and even travertine, to bring home for landscaping or small projects. The prices are listed in the office where visitors need to check in.
3700 Camino Del Llano
Belen, NM 87002
(505) 864-6300
http://www.nmtravertine.com/

BIBO

The mix of people who sought their fortunes in New Mexico included Jews from Eastern Europe fleeing their repressive governments. The story of the Bibo brothers is one of the more unusual stories with one of the brothers becoming the only non-Native American governor of the Acoma Pueblo.

Nathan and Simon Bibo left Germany and arrived in Santa Fe in the early 1860s. They became merchants and were soon joined by their 16-year-old brother Solomon.

Over the years Solomon Bibo developed ties with the Acoma people including marrying Juana Valle, the granddaughter of the Acoma governor, Martin Valle, in 1875. Bibo also established the first trading post on Acoma Pueblo land. That led to a political battle with the Indian Agent in charge of the Acoma Pueblo. The Acoma people themselves allied with Solomon, going as far as electing him as their governor in

1885, first and perhaps only, non-Indian governor of the Acoma Pueblo.

His passion for education led him to open up new educational opportunities for the people of pueblo. But not everyone liked the government schools and Bibo was caught up in the dissension.

By 1920 Bibo, Juana and their children were living in San Francisco. Solomon Bibo died in 1934, and Juana died in March 1941. Many of the Bibo descendants lived out their lives in New Mexico.

The town of Bibo was named after the brothers, which is a bit of an oddity since there is no evidence that the brothers actually lived there. Further, the **Bibo Bar** also has no connection to the Bibo family. It was started in 1913 by Joseph Hanosh whose family originated in Lebanon.

The bar has become a popular destination presided over by Hanosh's grandson, current owner Edward Michael. It's a stop on the Green Chile Trail, and serves New Mexican specialties including their excellent quesadillas, in the friendly, community bar and restaurant.
Bibo, NM 87014
(505) 552-9428

COCHITI PUEBLO

Located 55 miles north of Albuquerque and 35 miles south of Santa Fe, The Cochiti Pueblo is located on over 53,000 acres. The Pueblo de Cochiti offers visitors an 18-hole golf course. The town of Cochiti Lake is the site of the Cochiti Reservoir. In the land of little water, the 1.2 square-mile reservoir, built for flood control of the Rio Grande, offers sailing, windsurfing, kayaking, and fishing (depending on water levels). There is a swim beach and playground. In addition, visitors are welcome to view the pueblo's traditional dances.

Learn more about visiting Cochiti Lake:
http://www.recreation.gov/recreationalAreaDetails.do?contractCode=NRSO&recAreaId=485

SPECIAL FOCUS: STORYTELLERS

Storytellers are such an integral part of Native American artisan crafts that it's hard to believe there was a time before these iconic figures existed. But unlike woven baskets and clay pots that stretch back for eons, storytellers are a recent creation. Master potter Helen Cordero (1915 – 1994) of the Cochiti Pueblo fused Cochiti figurative pottery and its storytelling tradition.

She recalls being inspired, in 1964, to shape that first clay figure of her grandfather telling stories to his five grandchildren. She made several to bring with her to a Santo Domingo feast day. Alexander Girard (1907 – 1993), a New York designer who collected folk art, was enchanted by the figures, buying all the "little people" and asking her to make larger seated figures with children. The Storyteller was an instant success. And the new tradition grew and grew.

Helen Cordero went on to create a rich diversity of figures, as did the potters in pueblos across the state. You can find storytellers who are human (male and female) as well as frogs, owls, turtles, even kangaroos. Some figures have only a couple of children while others are quite covered in tiny listeners.

You can find these beguiling figures everywhere across New Mexico, especially wherever Native American pottery is sold. They vary wildly in style and price, but they are one of the most charming developments in the field of pottery.

A great source of information on the early years of storytellers is The Pueblo Storyteller by Barbara Babcock and Guy and Doris Monthan.

CORRALES

In a desert, if you see green, there's likely to be water close by. It's the proximity to acequias (irrigation ditches) off the Rio Grande that has turned this village just northwest of Albuquerque into a tiny oasis, with horses, pastures, and orchards with the watermelon mountains of the Sandias

(Sandia means watermelon in Spanish) in the background. Then, add art and restaurants, and you have Corrales.

The wine-growing tradition in New Mexico began with Spanish colonization and the need for sacramental wine. Today this tradition has expanded beyond the original "mission grapes" and is upheld by the Corrales Wine Loop, which welcomes wine lovers to their tasting rooms. All of the current Loop wineries offer a regular schedule that includes Saturdays and Sundays (although the exact hours may vary), making it enticingly easy to start at one end of town and sip (responsibly) to the other. Note that they may have seasonal hours.

Acequia Winery derives its name from the old Spanish term for the irrigation canals that channel water from the Rio Grande River.
240 Reclining Acres
Corrales, NM 87048
(505) 264-1656
http://acequiawinery.com/

Corrales Winery offers the distinction of being a solar-powered winery, but those who choose to have a glass of wine can enjoy striking views of the Sandias from their patio.
6275 Corrales Road
Corrales, NM 87048
(505) 898-5165
http://corraleswinery.com/

Pasando Tiempo is the newest member of the Loop.
277 Dandelion Road
Corrales, NM 87048
(505) 228-0154
http://www.pasandotiempowinery.com/

The last winery, **Matheson Winery** is technically outside the town but still part of the winery collective.
103 Rio Rancho Blvd.
Rio Rancho, NM 87124
(505) 350-6557
http://www.mathesonwines.com/

Milagro Vineyards & Winery is not part of the wine loop; tours and tastings are available by appointment.
125 Old Church Road
Corrales, NM 87048
(505) 898-3998
http://www.milagrowine.com/

There's not a chain restaurant in sight in this local-focused town. Instead, there are individually owned and operated eateries serving everything from pizza to fine cuisine. Between them you can go from early breakfasts all the way to late-night brews.

There are two standout places to eat in Corrales. **Hannah & Nate's** is a beloved place for breakfast and lunch on their tree-shaded patio or in the air-conditioned dining areas.
4512 Corrales Road
Corrales, NM 87048
(505) 898-2370
http://www.hannahandnates.com/

When you crave fine dining with a laid-back vibe, **Indigo Crow** is a perfect choice with lunch and dinner and a Sunday brunch on their tree-shaded patio or by the fireplace in winter. They have recently opened a branch in Cave Creek, Arizona. Call to make reservations (recommended for dinner).
4515 Corrales Road
Corrales, NM 87048
(505) 898-7000

If the galleries and shops aren't enough of a reason to visit, **La Entrada Park** (by the Community Library at 84 W La Entrada Road) is a patch of cooling green grass.

The Corrales Society of Artists runs the yearly Art in the Park the first Sunday in June, August, September and October. Find more information at: **http://nmartistsmarket.org/**

The **Corrales Growers Market** adds live music to the baked goods, jams, honey, and locally grown seasonal fruits and vegetables.
500 Jones Road at the corner of Corrales Road
http://corralesgrowersmarket.com/

Wagner Farms, an agricultural institution for one hundred years, has its own farm stand and special events.
5000 Corrales Road
Corrales, NM 87048
https://www.facebook.com/Wagnerfarms/

Although no longer a place of worship, **the Old San Ysidro Church** still welcomes the townspeople. The Corrales Historical Society restored and now maintains the iconic Old Church dating back to 1868 (and listed on the New Mexico Register of Cultural Properties and the National Register of Historic Places). They offer an enticing program of activities that are listed on their website.
966 Old Church Road
Corrales, NM 87048
(505) 897-1513
http://www.corraleshistory.org/

ESTANCIA

It's only one day a year, but this tidy welcoming town has hosted a Pumpkin Chunkin' event every October for over eighteen years. The town's Arthur Park also shelters something rare in New Mexico—a small-town lake.
http://townofestancia.com/index.php?page=special-events

JEMEZ SPRINGS

The village and the Jemez Valley are known for its informal hot springs and the Jemez State Monument.

Jemez State Monument is the site of an abandoned pueblo and its mission church built in the 1300s. Today, the ruins of the pueblo and the mission lie just outside the town of Jemez Springs. There is a quarter-mile interpretive trail that gives folks access to the ruins.
State Highway 4
Jemez Springs, NM 87025
(575) 829-3530
http://nmmonuments.org/jemez

The **Jemez Pueblo** itself is still in existence, but is generally closed to visitors, although the Walatowa Visitor Center provides information about the history and culture of the Jemez people.
7413 Highway 4
Jemez Pueblo, NM 87024
(575) 834-7235
http://www.jemezpueblo.com/

As suggested by the name, this area is famous for its hot springs. Lists of lodging (some associated with hot springs) can be found at http://www.jemezsprings.org/lodging.html

The Jemez Springs Bath House is owned and operated by the Village of Jemez Springs. The profit goes back into the village.
62 Jemez Springs Plaza
Jemez Springs, NM 87025
http://www.jemezsprings.org/hotsprings.html

MORIARTY

In 1887 Michael Moriarty, his wife, and three children arrived in the Estancia Valley and began ranching. By 1903, enough people lived there to need a post office and Moriarty became the first postmaster. Around the same time the railroad came through and established a station by the Moriarty ranch. And the town Moriarty was born.

Moriarty flourished until the rail boom went bust. Then Route 66 arrived, revitalizing the town. Although the first alignment did little good, in 1937 the Mother Road straightened out and bestowed on the town all the benefits that being on the Main Street of America offered.

Schwebach Farm Market, open from late July until mid-October, is a multi-generational family farm that offers its own farm-grown produce. Open Monday through Saturday, you can check their website for the produce currently being harvested. They grow everything from apples to winter squash.
807 W. Martinez Road
Moriarty, NM 87035
(505) 832-6171
http://www.schwebachfarm.com/

This Route 66 town offers two antique places that are close enough to make a great double-header for a trip.

Overseen by Archie Lewis, the **Lewis Antique Auto and Toy Museum** is a fascinating graveyard of old cars—some truly antique—in various states of genteel decay. Inside are the pride-and-joy cars in beautiful condition. There's also Lewis's collection of toys and trains. You'll visit to see these wonderful early automobiles—regardless of their condition. About 600 bits and pieces of cars fill the yard, including Model A and Model T Fords. The museum is generally open, and Archie Lewis is usually around to chat. Although there is no admission fee, donations are appreciated.
905 US Route 66 East
Moriarty, NM 87035
(505) 832-6131

> **Did You Know...**
>
> **A Beloved Cartoon Character Is Also Our State Bird?**
>
> The roadrunner is found throughout the state and is a form of ground cuckoo. Although generally flightless, it can run up to twenty miles per hour and can run down prey. Roadrunners eat small animals like mice and lizards, insects, and even small birds. The Road Runner was part of a cartoon pair (along with Wile E. Coyote), but the real thing looks and acts very differently from the cartoon version.

Southwest Soaring Museum is right down the road and houses all things soaring related, and a couple that aren't. The museum does have regular hours, but they change with the season.
Call to check hours.
918 Historic US 66
Moriarty, NM 87035
(505) 832-9222
http://www.swsoaringmuseum.org/Whats_new.htm

MOUNTAINAIR

Like so many towns in New Mexico, Mountainair started out as a railroad town, but it soon became famous as the Pinto Bean

Capital of the US. They were the largest grower and processor of this food staple. Years of drought ended that crop, but the resilient little town morphed into a ranching community. As the drought continued, ranching became a bit precarious. Although, economically, Mountainair has seen better days, there are some unique places to visit.

Everyone needs a hardware store, but **Gustin Hardware** is also a repository for the Gustin family's collection of mounted and stuffed animals. One of the family members was a taxidermist and the animals can be found throughout the store.
117 W Broadway
Mountainair, NM 87036
(505) 847-2261

Every prosperous town also had at least one hotel, and in 1923, the **Shaffer Hotel** opened in Mountainair. It was the Art Deco era with rich colors, bold geometric shapes, and artistic embellishments. The ever individualistic Southwest had its own version. Pueblo Deco was whipping through the landscape. The Shaffer art and architecture is an idiosyncratic mix that works. The hotel is still open to guests.
103 West Main St.
Mountainair, NM 87036
(505) 847-2998
http://www.shafferhotel.com

Head one mile south out of town to **Rancho Bonito**. Once owned by Shaffer and his family, it is now closed, but it remains a stellar example of American Folk Art and an intriguing photo op. The building is also listed on the National Register of Historical Places.

Three national monuments in the area make up **Salinas Pueblo Missions National Monument**, bound together by their shared history of the Spanish and Pueblo early encounters.

There are no regularly scheduled tours at **Salinas Pueblo Missions,** but if you call in advance you can arrange for a guided tour by one of the park rangers. This map helps

visitors locate the sites:
http://www.nps.gov/sapu/planyourvisit/things2know.htm

Abó is the site of the seventeenth-century Mission of San Gregoiro de Abó. There are also petroglyphs in the area and the park rangers offer tours if you call in advance. The ruins are one-half mile north of US 60 on NM 513. (505) 847-2400.

Gran Quivira is the largest of the sites, spread over 600 acres. At one time, this was a city with several pueblos within its area. Today, there's only one available to explore. Mound 7, built between 1400 and 1500 AD, was excavated, unearthing a total of 226 rooms, and the remains of an even earlier circular pueblo. Most of the rooms have been backfilled as the best way to preserve the delicate structures. There is an interpretative trail, a museum with some of the artifacts, and one room left open for viewing. From the Visitor Center in Mountainair, the ruins are 26 miles south on NM 55. (505) 847-2770.

Quarai contains the best preserved of the mission churches. Completed around 1629, Quarai also has Spanish Inquisition history, having served as the church's headquarters for the notorious Inquisition in New Mexico. The pueblo and the mission were finally abandoned in 1674, as a result of drought and Apache attacks. From the Visitor Center in Mountainair, the ruins are eight miles north on NM 55 and one mile west. (505) 847-2290

SANDIA PARK (SEE ALSO SANDIA CREST)

Located in the mountains just outside of Albuquerque, the community is one of several along the Turquoise Trail (Scenic Route 14). It's green and rural and is home to two very special tourist opportunities.

The town of Sandia Park is located on the route up to Sandia Crest in the Cibola National Forest. Cibola National Forest covers more than 1.6 million acres, but one of its four Wilderness areas, the 37,200-acre Sandia Mountain Wilderness Area, abuts Albuquerque and some of its suburbs. One of the more spectacular drives is to take Route 14 north to NM 536 West and follow the road into the forest.

135

Tinkertown Museum is a folk art wonderland of miniature carved wooden figures, including an animated Western town and circus performers. This fantastical delight started with tinkerer Ross Ward, who loved carving miniature wood figures. Fascinated by the tiny villages, farms, and circuses he had seen growing up in the Midwest, Ward started with circus figures, and his collection just grew from there. Then, he tinkered some more and covered his original home with glass bottles.

Ward was also a talented artist. The Mineshaft Tavern in Madrid has one of his murals on display. Sadly, he died in 2002 at 57 after living several years with Alzheimer's disease. His wife keeps the seasonal folk art museum going. There's much more than tiny figures to entrance visitors, so stop by and explore.
121 Sandia Crest Road
Sandia Park, NM 87047
(505) 281-5233
http://tinkertown.com/

Sandia Park is also home to alpaca. It's hard to imagine how impossibly cute these furry four-foot-high creatures are until you see them in person. Big eyes, long lashes, curly fur—even shorn of their fleece they sport a topknot that makes them even more adorable.

Whispering Spirit Alpaca is run by Sandra and Lee Liggett, who turn the natural-colored alpaca fleece into felted (nonwoven) hand-sewn fashion items. The setting is pastoral with rolling hills and mountains in the background. The grounds are home to their herd of endearing fleecy alpaca.

The Liggetts welcome visitors—just make arrangements in advance via info@whispirit.net or phone (505) 286-8058. http://www.whispirit.net/home.html

---

TIJERAS

Another community nestled next to Albuquerque, Tijeras is also the site of an ancient, abandoned pueblo, located behind the Ranger Station. The pueblo has actually been abandoned twice. It was originally built in the early 1300s, but shortly thereafter its inhabitants left. Then, around 1390, a second wave rebuilt the pueblo, although on a much smaller scale. As with most of the abandoned settlements throughout the states making up the Four Corners, by 1425 the pueblo was abandoned permanently.

Little is known about the settlers except for pieces of their pottery and some other artifacts left behind.
Friends of the **Tijeras Pueblo** have set up an interpretive center. The hours may vary and visitors are advised to call to see if staff will be in the building. The interpretative trail, however, is always open.
Sandia Ranger Station
11776 Highway 337
Tijeras, NM 87059
(505) 281-3304
http://www.friendsoftijeraspueblo.org/welcomehomepage.html

SOUTHWEST

The vast open spaces of southwest New Mexico offer ghost towns, and small villages with surprising experiences. The Gila National Forest dominates this part of the state with all its outdoor attractions. This is a mineral-rich area and the towns often highlight their past and present mining. It's also home to some surprising high-tech attractions and events.

Several Native American groups inhabited southwest New Mexico in the years around 1000 AD.

Much of this area was home to the Mimbres people, known for their striking pottery. Its black-on-white designs often incorporated stylized animals and repeating geometric abstract designs and patterns.

They lived in the area at a roughly similar time frame as the Ancient Puebloans who had settled in the upper reaches of the state—the area known today as the Four Corners.

The Mimbres were considered part of the Mogollon group, named after the Mogollon Mountain Range that was their home. These names were not derived from anything known about the people themselves. Many of the names throughout New Mexico were bestowed by the Spanish. The Mimbres were the people who lived around the Mimbres River, named by the Spanish for the abundance of small willows, called mimbres, found along its banks. The mountain range was named for Juan Ignacio Flores Mogollon, governor between 1712 and 1715 of much of the area that today is New Mexico.

BAYARD (SEE ALSO SILVER CITY)

It wasn't only gold and silver that drew would-be miners to New Mexico. While those precious metals were lures, New Mexico also offered other treasures from underground, including coal and copper.

In 1910, open pit mining of copper began near the town of Santa Rita. Santa Rita is no more—it was razed when the open pit mines expanded. Today the mine is among the world's largest—1.5 miles wide and 1,500 feet deep. It's still growing as copper continues to be dug out of the earth.

Bayard is also the site of union history. It was there that a group of miners struck for the right to have a union, and recently it was the site where the miners voted to decertify that union.

In 1950, in the union hall in Bayard members of the International Union of Mine, Mill and Smelter Workers Local 890 (more succinctly called Mine Mill Local 890) voted to go on strike against the mine that was then owned by the Empire Zinc Co. The 15-month action, called the Salt of the Earth strike, forced Empire Zinc to grant better pay and working conditions for the mine's workers. The 1954 movie Salt of the Earth depicted that historic strike.

This is a trailer for the movie: https://youtu.be/l6Ro8dvYpsM

Salt of the Earth generated a flaming uproar when it was released, and it was banned during the McCarthy era. Today, it

138

is honored for its depiction of mining life. In 1992, the Library of Congress chose to list it in the National Film Registry as one of the films deemed "culturally, historically or aesthetically significant." The movie is now in the public domain, and you can watch it in several places on YouTube, or you can download it at:
https://archive.org/details/clacinonl_SaltOfTheEarth

In 2014 further union history was made when workers at the Chino Mine voted 236-83 to decertify the 72-year-old Local 890. The change in sentiment is attributed to improved mine safety and better wages.

Bayard Union Hall is also famous for its Salt of the Earth mural painted as part of the Youth Mural Program of the Mimbres Region Arts Council.
302 Tom Foy Blvd.
Bayard, NM 88023
http://mimbresarts.org/youth-mural-program

The Historical and Mining District Committee currently runs the **Historic Mining District Tour**. Tours begin at Bayard City Hall and cost five dollars. Call to reserve a seat on the tour bus. Tours run the second Tuesday of every month.
800 Central Ave.
Bayard, NM 88023
(575) 537-3327

CHLORIDE

An overnight boomtown of the silver variety, Chloride once boasted the requisite saloons, hotels, and even a newspaper. Today the few folks who make their home in 4Chloride, 40 miles west of Truth or Consequences, are finding that it is becoming a bit of a ghost town turned tourist destination.

Several of the old Chloride buildings along Wall Street are still standing. They house a local museum as well as gift shops and galleries. The Pioneer Store Museum has its own fascinating backstory—the James family walked away from it in 1923 fully stocked and intact, thinking their son would come and take it

139

over. He never did. After being bought by new owners, the building was restored, opening in 1998.
http://www.pioneerstoremuseum.com/

DEMING

Largely ignored by tourism, the Deming area is becoming known for its grape-growing—the result of its relatively mild winters. Deming also offers a historic downtown, and the city's website offers an online **walking tour guide**.
http://www.cityofdeming.org/visit-deming/walking-tour

Deming was named after Mary Ann Deming Crocker, wife of Charles Crocker, who founded the Central Pacific Railroad and was one of the major forces in building the transcontinental railway. There were actually two transcontinental railways. The first, built around 1869, ran from Iowa to the Pacific.

It was the second transcontinental that happened in Deming. Around 1881 or 1882, the Southern Pacific (which had also been acquired by Crocker and his partners) met the famed Atchison, Topeka, and Santa Fe Railway at Deming, connecting Atchison, Kansas to Los Angeles.

The famous Silver Spike was driven in Deming in 1881 to commemorate the meeting of those two lines. Although the decline in importance of the rail shipping and travel did irrevocable harm to the economy, the area is finding new life as a premier grape-growing region for the state.

The **St. Clair Winery** in Deming offers tours of their winery, the largest in New Mexico. The winery has an interesting history—six generations of winemakers. Hérve Lescombes started St. Clair in 1981. St. Clair's top varietals are Cabernet Sauvignon, Chardonnay, Moscato, Merlot, and Zinfandel. They offer special events throughout the year. Check their website for updates.
1325 De Baca Road
Deming, NM 88030
(866) 336-7357
http://www.stclairwinery.com/deming

The family behind the **Luna Rossa Winery** also has a wine-making background going back generations. Paolo D'Andrea, who founded the winery in 2001 with his wife Sylvia, was born and raised in the famed Friuli wine-growing region of Italy, coming from four generations of wine growers. You can visit their tasting room.
3710 West Pine St.
Deming, NM 88030
(575) 544-1160
http://www.lunarossawinery.com

The other reason to visit Deming is **Rockhound State Park**, which offers a unique pick-your-own for unusual rocks and even semiprecious gemstones.
http://www.stateparks.com/rock_hound.html

ELEPHANT BUTTE

Elephant Butte Lake State Park is New Mexico's largest state park, offering 200 miles of shoreline along with camping and RV sites. It also offers a marina, docks, and a ramp. As with just about all the bodies of water in New Mexico, it's a reservoir lake. This one was created by a dam that was constructed in 1916 across the Rio Grande. You won't find much in the way of trees, but the water is stocked with bass, and sandy beaches beckon walkers. Amenities include pontoon boat rentals as well as kayak and paddleboard rentals.
101 Highway 195
Elephant Butte, NM 87935
(575) 744-5923
http://www.emnrd.state.nm.us/SPD/elephantbuttelakestatepark.html

In December, Elephant Butte holds a Beachwalk Luminaria Festival and Floating Parade of Lights.
http://www.sierracountynewmexico.info/annual-event/luminaria-beachwalk/

Along with nearby Truth or Consequences, Elephant Butte is a pickup place for tours of **Spaceport America**. Tours are currently offered out of Space Place, incubator for future Spaceport America companies. They advise you follow the directions provided at: http://www.spaceplacenm.com/map

FAYWOOD

New Mexico has had a varied geological history. Ancient New Mexico saw periods of volcanic activity and mountain building, with periodic submersion under the early seas. Dinosaurs roamed the drying land and volcanic eruptions created fields of black and red volcanic rock.

Located between Deming and Silver City, the lure of Faywood is the **City of Rocks State Park**, formed of volcanic ash 35 million years ago. Wind and rain worked the blocks into fantastical formations, giving the City of Rocks its name. The columns rise as high as 40 feet and are separated by paths, creating the "city" effect.
327 Highway 61
Faywood, NM 88034
(575) 536-2800
http://www.emnrd.state.nm.us/SPD/cityofrocksstatepark.html

Explore these monolithic rocks through this aerial tour:
https://youtu.be/B78UEVHVXaI

FORT SELDEN

The fort was established in 1865 to protect travelers, merchants, and settlers traveling the El Camino Real de Tierra Adentro, the Royal Inland Road from Mexico City to Texas and New Mexico.

Its most famous group of soldier-protectors was the Buffalo Soldiers of the 25th Infantry. At the end of the Civil War, Black cavalry and infantry troops known as Buffalo Soldiers were sent to the American West. The term "buffalo soldier" is said to have come from the Native Americans who applied it to the Black troops because of their short curly hair and their courage and fortitude, much admired qualities of the buffalo.

Learn more about the Buffalo Soldiers of Fort Selden with this video: https://youtu.be/BWYAbRN4Kzw

The site was made a New Mexico State Monument in 1974 and is now preserved as a historic site by the Museum of New Mexico. There's an onsite visitor center with exhibitions and living history demonstrations on frontier and military life. The visitor center is open daily from 8:30 a.m. to 5:00 p.m., except Tuesday. Fort Selden Historic Site is located 13 miles north of Las Cruces, off I-25 at Exit 19.
http://www.nps.gov/nr/travel/El_Camino_Real_de_Tierra_Adentro/Fort_Selden.html

GLENWOOD

In 1889 silver and gold was discovered in the Mogollon Mountains just outside of Glenwood. Several mines were developed, and wagons hauled the ore to processing mills. The water needed to operate the mills came from a pipeline reaching up into the canyon.

The timber and iron bars that held the pipes to the rock walls needed frequent maintenance, and the workmen dubbed the system the Catwalk. Today it is the site of the one-mile Catwalk National Recreation Trail in the Gila National Forest, which follows the route of the old pipeline, clinging dramatically to the side of Whitewater Canyon hovering above Whitewater creek.
http://www.fs.usda.gov/recarea/gila/recarea/?recid=1998

Although it is currently closed as a result of heavy rain damage, the Catwalk is undergoing repairs. Call (575) 539-2481 for updates.

HATCH

About 40 miles from Las Cruces, Hatch is famous for its high-quality red and green chiles. New Mexicans are fiercely devoted to the fruit of the plants from the genus Capsicum and add green chile to just about everything from apple pies (surprisingly delicious) to pizza. New Mexicans believe there isn't a form of baked good (or anything cooked) that can't benefit from a shot of the state's chile.

143

Each year during chile season, dozens of vendors can be found lining the streets of Hatch, roasting the local chile. Actually, fall is chile roasting season everywhere in New Mexico, and the deliciously spicy aroma perfumes the air throughout the state. Hatch also has a famous Chile Festival every Labor Day Weekend. http://www.hatchchilefest.com/

SPECIAL FOCUS: NEW MEXICO CHILES

Chiles have been prized in the Americas across time as a source of both medicine and food.

From the mild bell pepper to hot jalapenos, all are the fruits of different varieties of Capsicum annuum. There are about twenty-seven species of Capsicum—about half of which we use today. Capsicum comes from the Greek kapos, "to bite;" although this may not describe the mild green pepper, almost all its relatives have a heat or bite that is legendary.

New Mexico's Own Chile

New Mexico has its own chile. The New Mexico chile was developed by pioneer New Mexican horticulturist Dr. Fabián Garcia in 1888—so it's no surprise that New Mexicans are wildly in love with their chile and add it to just about every dish. In fact, in New Mexico when you say you want green or red chile, it is assumed that it's New Mexican chile you are really requesting. Chile grown in the Hatch Valley is called Hatch chile, but it is New Mexican chile through and through.

Its flavor has been described as having a subtly sweet, spicy bite, but it can be anywhere from mild through very hot. Allowing the chile to ripen to red adds an earthiness to the flavor, but it will still deliver quite a tongue-burning punch. Some of the pueblos throughout the state grow their own variety with slightly different flavor and heat profiles.

A certification program was started in 2014—the New Mexico Certified Chile—attempting to certify the growing of New Mexico chile peppers. Accept no substitute for our beloved New Mexico chile.

By the way, in New Mexico, chile refers to the plant or fruit from the plant while the term chili refers to a culinary dish consisting of a meat, beans, tomatoes, and chile powder.

Feel the Burn
The heat comes mainly from an oily compound called capsaicin, and some varieties are so hot they can actually blister the skin. This leads to the sensible suggestion to wear gloves when preparing the hotter varieties and to NEVER touch delicate skin tissues, including your eyes, without thoroughly washing your hands.

Capsaicin, being oily, can't be diluted in water, so when your mouth is on fire, beer is said to be a better choice (and New Mexico loves its craft brewers), but a dairy product works the best. Remember the sour cream that is ubiquitous in restaurants? Think of it as a delicious fire extinguisher.

Measure the Burn
The heat of the chile is measured in Scoville units—a scale developed Wilbur Scoville in 1912. It is a measure of the concentration of capsaicin. The green bell pepper rates zero on the Scoville scale, the poblano (or ancho) pepper and the jalapeno rate 1,000 to 4,000, and the Hatch chile comes in at under 2,500 units depending on growing conditions. Habanero and Scotch bonnet start at 100,000 units. And if you really want to court death by capsaicin, the hottest pepper in the world tops two million Scoville units. The Carolina Reaper is currently considered to be the hottest, and it was bred for that level of burn-your-insides-out heat.

Hatch is also home to giants. These are the jumbo figures found throughout Hatch and include a huge pink pig, a giant rooster mounted on top of the GMC Suburban, and the A&W Root Beer Mama and Papa. The Giants are part **of Sparky's Burgers, Barbecue, and Espresso**, owner Teako Nunn's quest to enjoy himself and make Hatch just a bit more fun.
115 Franklin St.
Hatch, NM 87937
(Exit 41, one mile south on Highway 26/Franklin St.)
(575) 267-4222
http://sparkysburgers.com

HILLSBORO (SEE ALSO LAKE VALLEY AND KINGSTON)

The towns of Hillsboro, Kingston, and Lake Valley were born in the silver and gold of the Black Range Mountains—a magnet for would-be miners and wealth-seekers. All three towns still exist, but more as ghosts of their former selves.

Hillsboro was founded more on gold than silver and was spared the descent into ghost town status when the silver market collapsed. Ranching also provided some economic stability, but the economy still faltered.

The town's remaining historic buildings are spread out along NM 152. Hillsboro has two small historical museums and some rich bawdy history. Pick up Historic Hillsboro: A Walking Tour Guide at shops in town. You can also download this helpful brochure:
http://www.blackrange.org/The_Black_Range_Rag/Hillsboro.html

Its most famous resident was certainly Sadie Orchard. There are a few reasons why Ms. Orchard was an unusual character in the story of Hillsboro. While accounts of her life vary considerably, there is little doubt that she was an independent, indomitable woman living a life filled with ups and downs.

Glenda Riley's book Wild Women of the Old West presents a thoughtful description of life at the time and is a good look into what Sadie herself might have confronted. Different accounts have Sadie born in England (even speaking with an English accent), but Riley has determined that she was most likely born in Mills County, Iowa sometime around 1860.

All accounts agree that she was originally called Sarah Jane Creech, but soon became known as Sadie. Somewhere along the way she married James Orchard, and later, they appear to have been divorced.

According to Clay Vaden's 1936 interview with Sadie, she came to the Black Range area in 1886, where she was one of the few women stagecoach drivers. She and her husband drove the

stage line for fourteen years and had their own coaches and a wagon.
http://files.usgwarchives.net/nm/sierra/bios/sadieorchard.txt

Other tales of Sadie Orchard confirm that she had another wilder side, opening a brothel on Virtue Avenue in Kingston. When she moved to Hillsboro, she opened the Ocean Grove Hotel and the Orchard Hotel, which eventually became a brothel.

Financial setbacks followed, and Sadie died in her early 80s almost penniless. She was buried in Truth or Consequences, which was then known as Hot Springs.

Sadie herself has proved to be of enduring interest, the epitome of the woman of the Old West. Her story was made into an episode of Death Valley Days—Season 16, Episode 9 called "The Saga of Sadie Orchard." It first aired on January 13, 1968. Unfortunately, it's not available online.

Her Ocean Grove Hotel is now the **Black Range Museum**, open long weekends and by appointment. The exhibits focus on Sadie Orchard and her longtime cook and restaurant manager, Tom Ying.
3 Carro Lane
Hillsboro, NM 88042
(575) 895-5233
http://www.sierracountynewmexico.info/attractions/black-range-museum/

The **Hillsboro Historical Society** also runs a small museum on Main Street, open Friday, Saturday, and Sunday. Call for exact hours.
(575) 895-3321
http://www.hillsboronmhistory.info/

To reach Hillsboro, take Exit 63 from I-25 to Hillsboro/Highway 152 West for eighteen miles. Lake Valley is located south of Hillsboro on NM 27.

KINGSTON (SEE ALSO HILLSBORO AND LAKE VALLEY)

Although Kingston was the site of Sadie Orchard's first brothel there is little left of her history in this tiny community. But once upon a time it was a silver-driven town that was served by several stagecoach lines. There was even an opera house where the Lillian Russell Troupe was reported to have once performed.

Almost none of the old buildings are left, except for the 1884 historic **Percha bank building**, which is now a museum and artist gallery open weekends. Call for exact hours.
46 Main St.
Hillsboro, NM 88042
(575) 895-5652
http://www.sierracountynewmexico.info/attractions/percha-bank-museum-kingston/

There's also a B&B named the **Black Range Lodge** in a building that dates back to the 1880s, although the stone walls and log ceilings are a bit newer, going back to the 1930s.
119 Main St.
Hillsboro, NM 88042
(575) 895-5652
(800) 676-5622
http://www.blackrangelodge.com/

LAKE VALLEY (SEE ALSO HILLSBORO AND KINGSTON)

The town of Lake Valley, founded in 1878, had a vein of silver so pure it was said that miners could simply saw it off the wall. The silver is gone, but the remains of the town form the kernel of a visitor-friendly ghost town. The Bureau of Land Management restored the schoolhouse and chapel, and the other buildings have been stabilized to slow further deterioration.

The BLM provides trail guides for the interpretive walking tour at the schoolhouse. It's open year round, but closed Tuesdays and Wednesdays. Their brochure is available online.

LAS CRUCES (SEE ALSO ORGAN, MESILLA, AND WHITE SANDS MISSILE RANGE MUSEUM)

"The City of the Crosses" is the second-largest city in New Mexico with just over 100,000 residents. It was founded in 1849, but as with almost all of the state, it was home to Native Americans prior to its official founding.

Las Cruces was also part of the push-pull of the international politics of Spain, Mexico, and the United States. Even the Confederacy had nominal title in the area. Las Cruces was also part of the Camino Real—the Royal Road—from Mexico to north of Santa Fe, which made it an important part of the trade system.

The railroad helped the city prosper. It is said that when the railroad came through in 1881, the townspeople were so excited they filled wagons with garlands.

The nearby town of Messila turned down the chance to have the railroad go through their area, which meant that Las Cruces participated in the railroad rush of prosperity and became the county seat. The charming town of Messila stayed small and delightful and is now part of the Las Cruces Metropolitan area.

To learn more about the railroad's influence on Las Cruces, visit the **Las Cruces Railroad Museum** located in the historic depot.
351 N Mesilla St.
Las Cruces, NM 88005
(575) 647-4480
http://www.las-cruces.org/departments/community-and-cultural-services/museum-system/railroad-depot-museum

Las Cruces also boasts a historic theater. Dating back to 1926, the **Rio Grande Theatre** is still delighting arts patrons. It also hosts gallery shows of local artists.

149

211 N Main St.
Las Cruces, NM 88001
(575) 523-6403
http://www.riograndetheatre.com/

There's some quirky history in Las Cruces in the form of the **Shalam Colony** founded by a New York dentist and doctor named John Newbrough. Newbrough wrote a new Bible (purportedly under divine instruction) that contained the Book of Shalam, which directed the group to gather and raise outcast and orphaned children according to strict religious principles. They were to be the spiritual leaders of a new age.

The colony was established in 1884 and managed to survive until Newbrough's early death from influenza in 1891. Several years of struggle followed, but in 1901 the children who had not been adopted were sent to other orphanages, and the colony came to an end. The Shalam Colony historic marker can be found at NM 185 at milepost 5.5.

But to really go back in time, think extinct creatures. New Mexico was once the playground of dinosaurs, and **Prehistoric Trackways National Monument** protects 280-million-year-old fossil footprints and trackways from extinct animals. Edaphosaurus (which has been translated into either Ground Lizard, or the more colorful Pavement Lizard) lived 280 to 300 million years ago. This large plant eater also sported a bony sail on its back. Dimetrodon (meaning Two Measures of Teeth) had an even bigger sail, and its diet leaned more heavily on meat and fish.

Finding the site and seeing the tracks can be quite a challenge. The Bureau of Land Management (BLM) notes: "The fossil sites are not marked and not easy to find." Check their website or call for tours and access information.
(575) 525-4300
http://www.blm.gov/nm/trackways

One of the culinary staples of New Mexico is chile, and Las Cruces is home to the **Chile Pepper Institute**. Open from June to October, the Chile Pepper Teaching Garden educates visitors about the beloved crop. The garden has over 150 different varieties of chile peppers, including the main species of

150

Capsicum (C. annuum, C. baccatum, C. chinense, and C. frutescens), from the mildest bell to the hottest habanero.

Visitors are welcome to visit the garden on their own. Self-guided maps are free and are available in a mailbox at the front of the garden. You can also arrange for a guided tour, but reservations must be made at least 48 hours in advance.
104 West University Ave.
Las Cruces, NM 88005
(575) 646-3028
http://www.chilepepperinstitute.org/chile_pepper_institute_garden_tour.php

Held for over 30 years, the **Whole Enchilada Fiesta** which had drawn visitors to Las Cruces has been retired. It started in 1980 with a six-foot enchilada and grew to a huge 10 1/2-foot-diameter enchilada, certified by Guinness World Records as the world's largest. But the Fiesta was a labor of love and when enchilada-maker Roberto Estrada decided to retire following his world record achievement, the board of the TWEF decided it was time to retire the event as well.

Although not considered a wine area, Deming winery **Luna Rossa** has their winery and pizzeria in Las Cruces (in addition to their tasting room in Deming).
1321 Avenida de Mesilla
Las Cruces, NM 88005
(575) 526-2484
http://www.lunarossawinery.com/contact

LORDSBURG

About 50 miles west of Deming (and a couple of miles from Lordsburg) is one of the state's ghost towns turned tourist attraction.

The town of **Shakespeare** had an up-and-down history, propelled from a watering hole and stagecoach stop into a town called Ralston as a result of a silver strike in 1870. A diamond swindle (salting the ground with diamonds to lure investors) dashed its fortunes in 1874.

151

The town's name was changed to Shakespeare in 1879 in an attempt to provide a fresh start with a name that was not associated with the scandalous swindle. About the same time, a new silver strike caused a brief revival, but the town faltered in 1893.

That year saw the Depression of 1893, part of a worldwide economic crisis of the early 1890s, which caused massive unemployment and the bankruptcy of about a quarter of the nation's railroads.

Perhaps even more devastating to the economy of the town and the area was the repeal of the Sherman Silver Purchase Act. This short-lived act was passed in 1890 and required the government to buy millions of ounces of silver, providing quite a boon to the mining industry. It was repealed in 1893, and silver mining never recovered.

Shakespeare is now owned by the Hill family, who open up the town one weekend a month for guided tours. They also have Living History reenactments four weekends a year. There are no onsite facilities, so feel free to bring a picnic lunch. Check their website and call for updates.
P.O. Box 253
Lordsburg, NM 88045
(505) 542-9034
http://www.shakespeareghostown.com/

MAGDALENA (SEE ALSO SOCORRO)

New Mexico's wide-open spaces and clear air have made the state a perfect place for astronomical stargazing. The high desert town of Magdalena at the edge of the Cibola National Forest has capitalized on this and offers **Enchanted Skies Star Parties.** Usually held twice a year in April and October, the event is sponsored by Magdalena Chamber of Commerce. Find out more at: http://enchantedskies.org/index.php

Magdalena is also the location of the **Very Large Array Visitor Center**, but the town offers no visitor facilities. The nearest place to stay is in Socorro.

Old Highway 60
Magdalena, NM 87825
https://public.nrao.edu/tours/visitvla

MESILLA (SEE ALSO LAS CRUCES)

The small charming town of Mesilla (it means Little Tableland) is a suburb of Las Cruces and still has its historic welcoming downtown plaza surrounded by shops and restaurants. The plaza is a perfect backdrop for the festivals and special events.

The historic Fountain Theatre opened in 1905. The name comes from the Fountain family, who have lived in Mesilla for generations. The theater is known for the 1870s facade and 1920s vintage murals. Its new owner, Tom Hutchinson, recently gave the building a restoration and upgrade. Its murals have been restored; new heating, ventilation, and air-conditioning systems have been added, among other upgrades. The **Fountain Theatre** reopened in February 2014.
2469 Calle de Guadalupe
Mesilla, NM 88005
(575) 524-8287
http://www.mesillavalleyfilm.org/

The city is also the site of Civil War history. The First Battle of Mesilla was fought on July 25, 1861. It was a Confederate victory and eventually Mesilla became the capital of the Confederate Arizona Territory. A second fight in 1862, called the Second Battle of Mesilla, ended in a Union victory and the withdrawal of Confederate troops.

Enjoy a minute of Mesilla at: https://youtu.be/9zIdGXz2iXI

MOGOLLON

Mogollon is a former mining town started in 1876 when gold was discovered.

They like to call themselves the Ghost Town That Refuses to Die and have a website with some of their history and places to visit. Note that this is a town that is open seasonally (if it opens

153

at all). So plan your visit accordingly, and check their website for information. According to their website, they became a ghost town in 1942.
http://www.mogollonenterprises.com/index.html

PIE TOWN

If you're thinking Pie Town is known for its pies, you'd be correct. Its name comes from the famous bakery products of Clyde Norman, who developed quite a reputation in the 1920s for his dried-apple pies. Of course, the backstory, as with much of the stories of the state, involves mining.

Did You Know...

New Mexico Was the First State to Have a State Cookie?

The biscochito is a small anise-flavored cookie which was brought to New Mexico by the early Spaniards. The cookie is used during special celebrations, wedding receptions, baptisms, the Christmas season, and during other holidays. It was made the state cookie in 1989.

Norman came to the area to claim his share of its gold and silver, but his mine never produced, so he opened a small store selling sundries, including pies made from dried apples.

This area was also cattle country, so both the cowboys and the miners would come into town for that sweet treat.

The tough economy of the Depression and the drought affected the ranchers, eventually causing the town to falter—until Russell Lee showed up.

Lee, a photographer for the Farm Security Administration of the US government, came to Pie Town and made the town and its people famous. He snapped around 600 photographs documenting the townspeople and their way of life during the Great Depression. You can see some of these historic photos at http://www.blm.gov/nm/st/en/prog/more/cultural_resources/homesteads_in_new/pie_town_homesteaders.html

The town has reinvented itself based on the pie legacy of Clyde Norman. The best time to visit is in September when the town hosts its **Pie Town Pie Festival.**
http://www.pietowncouncil.com/pf_home.html

If you miss the festival, you can still enjoy some pie perched atop the Continental Divide.

Several places in town are open seasonally.
Pie-O-Neer Café
US-60
Pie Town, NM 87827
(575) 772-2711
http://www.pie-o-neer.com/

Pie Town Café
US-60
Mile Marker 56
Pie Town, NM 87827
(505) 772-2700
http://www.pietown.com/

The **Pie Source** is another pie-focused business and is located in an unusual building—a period authentic homestead cabin decorated with memorabilia from the families, homesteaders, and ranchers of the 1920s. You can also admire their windmill collection while you enjoy the pie.
US-60
Pie Town, NM 87827
Bakery (575) 772-2919
Homestead Pie and Coffee Bar (760) 420-9714
http://www.thepiesource.com/

PINON

In the realm of trivia, here's a question—is there a New Mexico town named after a nut? The answer is yes. The town of Pinon was named in 1907 by local schoolteacher John W. Nations (himself having a bit of an interesting name) after the piñon pine trees in the area.

The nuts are highly prized in New Mexico for their gentle flavor with a hint of sweetness. They are made into cookies, dropped into pancakes, and added to chocolate candy. They are also phenomenally expensive due to the infrequent flowering of the pinon pine tree and the labor involved in gathering them.

The town itself is a ranching community located at the southwest edge of Lincoln National Forest between Artesia and Alamogordo, south of Route 82.

PINOS ALTOS (SEE ALSO SILVER CITY)

Historic Pinos Altos, six miles north of Silver City on NM 15, calls itself the mining ghost town that still thrives. The legend goes that two would-be gold miners stopped to take a drink at Bear Creek and discovered that lustrous elusive ore. Several of the old buildings from the mid-1800s still line Main Street. http://www.pinosaltos.org/

One reason to make a stop is the circa 1860 **Buckhorn Saloon**. Although it has been renovated, it still maintains that disreputable look and offers live music several nights a week.
32 Main St.
Pinos Altos, NM 88053
(575) 538-9911
http://www.buckhornsaloonandoperahouse.com

QUEMADO

Although you can't just drop in and visit, Walter De Maria's 1977 art installation The Lightning Field is located near Quemado.

The installation is made of 400 stainless steel poles arranged in a grid. The only way you get to see the installation is if you book an overnight stay in advance. Photography is not permitted. They start taking reservations for the year on February 1. You can make your reservations through their website.
3469 US-60
Quemado, NM 87829
(505) 898-3335
http://www.diaart.org/sites/page/56/1301

RADIUM SPRINGS (SEE FORT SELDEN)

The connection between the fort and the name of the town came from the story that soldiers enjoyed dipping in the area's hot springs. When an analysis of the water revealed sufficient concentration of radium, the town's name was changed to highlight their unique water. The Radium Springs Inn (which may also have been known by various names including Fort Selden Hot Springs Resort, Bailey's Bath House, O'Dell's Hot Springs Hotel, the Lodge at Radium Springs, Radium Hot Springs Inn, and Leasburg Hotel) was originally built around 1930 by the Santa Fe Railroad, perhaps as a Harvey House. But its long history has not been one of success. Bad luck seems to have visited and stayed. The inn now has a new owner whose plans for the property are not yet determined.

RESERVE

This is one of the places people stumble upon by finding a statue and a plaque and wondering what happened there. Now called Reserve, it is the site where Elfego Baca held off a gang of Texas cowboys who wanted to kill him.

In October 1884, in the town of Lower San Francisco Plaza (now Reserve, New Mexico) located within the Gila National Forest, Elfego Baca arrested a drunken cowboy named Charlie McCarty. Baca flashed his badge at McCarty and took his gun. McCarty's fellow cowboys were not happy about this and tried to rescue their friend. Accounts differ, but Baca eventually had to take refuge in a nearby house. The number of attackers varies between 40 and 80, depending on the source, pegged at 40 (by the villagers) or 80 (as Elfego claimed).

Allegedly, the cowboys fired more than 4,000 shots into the house, until the adobe building was full of holes. Baca returned fire, supposedly killing at least four men. Incredibly, Baca survived. He eventually surrendered and was brought to trial for the shooting. But he was acquitted, so the story goes, when the door of the house was entered as evidence—with more than 400 bullet holes in it. The incident became known as the Frisco Shootout. Walt Disney's Wonderful World of Color Season 5, Episode 1 brought the story to television as

"The Nine Lives of Elfego Baca" that aired on October 3, 1958. Robert Loggia played Baca.

Here's a link to the YouTube video of the episode: https://www.youtube.com/watch?v=TPQwYgEZCnI

SAN ANTONIO (SEE ALSO SOCORRO)

Located at the edge of Bosque del Apache—one of the state's most popular wildlife refuges—there's not much to see in the town itself. But it does have a claim to fame. While still part of the New Mexico Territory, San Antonio was the birthplace of Conrad Hilton in 1887. His father, Augustus Halvorsen Hilton, emigrated from Norway and was said to have owned a very successful general store. Later on, Conrad started working in his father's store, eventually taking over the management. When New Mexico became a state in 1912, Hilton was elected to the state legislature.

Bosque del Apache National Wildlife Refuge is a 57,191-acre birding refuge. While it looks like an area of spectacular natural beauty, one of the reasons for its success is that the Bosque is actively managed to mimic the natural ebb and flow of the Rio Grande. The flooded marshes provide an environment that encourages a large visiting avian population, and the folks who love to watch (and photograph) them. See why people love visiting Bosque del Apache with this beautiful video: https://youtu.be/UnkGFrkTgus

Although San Antonio is the closest town to Bosque del Apache, there's no lodging in town and there are few dining options. Socorro, 20 miles away, offers a nicely diverse offering of rooms and places to eat.

SILVER CITY (SEE ALSO BAYARD, PINOS ALTOS)

Named after the valuable metal found in its hills, Silver City gained a railroad station in 1881 and a university (Western New Mexico University) in 1893.

The town of Santa Clara (this is not the same as the Santa Clara Pueblo) is famous for its proximity to Fort Bayard, but Silver

City is a better choice for lodging and restaurants. The historic fort is located just a few minutes from Silver City on Highway 180.

This was an area of contention between the Native American tribes and the miners and settlers, so in 1866, the US Army built Fort Bayard as protection. **Fort Bayard** was established by troops of Company B, 125th United States Colored, part of the legendary Buffalo Soldiers. A memorial to the Buffalo Soldiers was erected in 1992 in the middle of the field.

The fort lasted until 1899, but rather than closing, as had other forts across the territory, Fort Bayard became a sanatorium, and years later a veterans' hospital.

Over the years, buildings were added or upgraded. But eventually the site became unwanted. It was a large complex without a clear function, and one that still needed maintenance.

In 1965, the State of New Mexico took responsibility for the buildings and its 484 acres. It resumed life as a center for varied medical programs. The 16-acre cemetery dating back to the fort's establishment became the Fort Bayard National Cemetery.

Through the efforts of the Fort Bayard Historic Preservation Society, the fort was named a New Mexico Historic District and a National Historic Landmark in 2004.

Fort Bayard Historic Preservation Society offers tours and special events.
(575) 388-4477
http://www.fortbayard.org
https://www.facebook.com/fortbayardhistoricpreservationsociety

The people of the Mongollon culture (named by the Spanish after that mountain range) lived in natural caves as well as in settlements along the Gila River. **Gila Cliff Dwellings National Monument** shelters several of those dwellings. Although it is open every day, the trail to the Gila Cliff Dwellings is only open until 4:00 p.m. Everyone must be off the trail by 5:00 p.m. It takes about two hours to drive to the monument from Silver City. http://www.nps.gov/gicl/index.htm

Here's a video created by the Youth in Park Rangers of the National Park Service. If you can't get there to visit, or want to know what you'll be seeing, this is an excellent introduction. https://youtu.be/DgxKrUFMhEM

As with any historic town, Silver City is proud of its 500-seat Liberty Theater, first opened in 1923. It was re-named the **Silco Theater** to reflect the economy of the town (SILver-COpper). Fortunes changed as the mines played out and the theater eventually closed.

The Silver City MainStreet Project is currently raising funds to renovate the Silco Theater. You can follow their progress on the website and check out the building as it undergoes renovation.
311 N Bullard St.
Silver City, NM 88061
(575) 534-9005
http://www.silvercitymainstreet.com/index.php/projects/the-silco-theater

Western New Mexico University Museum is home to one of the world's most comprehensive collections of Mimbres pottery and basketry. The Mimbres were the people who lived around the Mimbres River, named by the Spanish for the abundance of small willows found along its banks—mimbres. In addition to Mimbres pottery, the museum includes pieces by world-famous San Ildefonso potters, Maria and Julian Martinez.
1000 W College Ave.
Silver City, NM 88061
(575) 538-6386
http://www.wnmumuseum.org/

A restored 1881 Italianate building is home to the **Silver City Museum.** H B Ailman House collection includes about 50,000 objects relating to the peoples and history of southwest New Mexico, including 20,000 photographs. Assaying equipment, mining gear, and office equipment from the Santa Rita,

Tyrone, and other mines in the Grant County area are also on display.
312 W Broadway
Silver City, NM 88061
Four blocks west of Hwy 90
(575) 538-5921
(877) 777-7947 (out-of-town only)
http://www.silvercitymuseum.org/index.html

When you're thirsty, Silver City is home to one of the new distilleries in the state. The smallest in terms of production, **Little Toad Creek Brewery & Distillery** offers a surprisingly large variety to tempt spirit-lovers in the southwest corner of New Mexico. The distillery handcrafts vodka, rum, whiskey, and a variety of liqueurs in small batches. They are particularly excited about their Green Chili Vodka, which they swear makes the world's best Bloody Mary. In addition, they offer white and spiced rum along with aged whiskey. A complete eating and drinking destination, they offer beers, wines, and pub food as well as special events.
200 N. Bullard St.
Silver City, NM 88061
(575) 956-6144
http://littletoadcreekbrewerydistillery.com/

Finally, Silver City hosts a yearly **Silver City Wild West Pro Rodeo.** You can see bull riding, fast riding, and roping as well as the ever-adorable Mutton Busting, in which children ages five or six attempt to "bust" sheep. It's not that the sheep are wild; they just want to dislodge the pint-size rider on their backs. http://silvercityprorodeo.com/

SOCORRO (SEE ALSO SAN ANTONIO AND MAGDALENA)

The area of Socorro was once home to the people of the Teypana Pueblo. In 1598, a group of Spanish under the leadership of Don Juan de Onate (who was attempting to colonize the area for Spain) arrived hungry and short of provisions. Luckily they found the Teypana, who provided them with badly needed corn. The grateful Spanish named the village Socorro (derived from the verb to aid, or to succor).

Details of the Teypana history are scarce. It is believed that by the time of the Pueblo Revolt in 1680, there was little left of their culture. But it is clear that they did not participate in the revolt and those remaining left with the Spanish for Mexico. Even the location of their pueblo seemed to have vanished.

In the 1980s, archaeologist Michael Marshall discovered a large 200-250 room pueblo about seven miles south of Socorro, believed to have been the Teypana Pueblo. Although it was on private land, the owners gave permission for the excavation, requiring only that the artifacts recovered and knowledge gained were placed on public display in Socorro County.

That stipulation has been honored, and the result is an exhibit at the Camino Real Center. But the archaeological site itself does not exist anymore. Following the excavation, all rooms were back-filled—as is the standard practice to protect the remains from further damage and allow future investigations.

The **El Camino Real Historic Trail Site Visitor's Center and Museum** is about 30 miles south of Socorro. Turn off at Exit 115. The center and museum is currently open Wednesday through Sunday.
(575) 854-3600
http://www.elcaminoreal.org

The story of the Teypana is tied to the story of one of the oldest Catholic churches in the United States. **San Miguel Mission Church** was founded in 1598 by two Franciscan priests who had been accompanying Don Juan de Onate. The priests decided to stay in the area and build a small church, enlarged between the years 1615 and 1626 and embellished with carvings and silver. The mission was abandoned during the Pueblo Revolt, and it wasn't until the early 1800s that the structure was rebuilt.
403 El Camino Real
Socorro, NM 87801
(575) 835-2891
http://www.sdc.org/~smiguel/index.php

In addition to its history, Socorro is a popular destination because of its technology and its Dark Skies participation.

The **Very Large Array** is another Socorro area attraction, although the Visitor Center is actually in the town of Magdalena. While much of New Mexico is steeped in history, the VLA is one area in which the state is truly cutting edge. It is the site of one of the world's finest astronomical radio observatories, with 27 radio antennas in a Y-shaped configuration on the Plains of San Agustin, 50 miles west of Socorro, New Mexico.

In addition to the photo opportunity presented by the VLA, there are regular guided tours of the facility the first Saturday of the month from the **Karl G. Jansky Very Large Array Visitor Center.**
Old Highway 60
Magdalena, NM 87825
https://public.nrao.edu/tours/visitvla

The city of Socorro coordinates its night stargazing program with the schedule of the VLA. After you visit the VLA, head over to visit the **Etscorn Observatory** on the campus of New Mexico Tech an hour after dusk for Guided Night Stargazing. Star buffs will want to check out the astronomy club seasonal monthly meetings at the Etscorn Observatory and other events open to the public. For further information, visit their website: http://infohost.nmt.edu/~astro/contact.html

The **Hammel Museum** building began as a brewery in the mid-1880s producing beer and ale. Business was quite successful until Prohibition in 1919 ended the production of alcoholic spirits. Hardly missing a beat, the business shifted to bottling soft drinks, finally becoming an ice house until it closed in the mid-1950s. Now the building is a museum focusing on early Socorro and the history of the brewing company. The current hours are limited to the first Saturday morning of each month. Private tours can be arranged by calling the Socorro County Historical Society.
500 6th St. N
Socorro, NM 87801
(575) 835-3183
http://socorronm.org/attractions/hammel-museum/

The **Mineral Museum** is open in the newly opened Headen Center, exhibiting minerals and rocks from the Las Cruces, Silver City, Bingham, Magdalena, Golden, Dixon, and Grants areas. The Headen Center is located at the SW corner of Bullock Blvd and Leroy Place. (575) 835-5140

Fort Craig Historic Site was established in 1854 to guard trade routes against Indian campaigns. During the Civil War, the fort became a Union Army outpost. Fort Craig was home to Buffalo Soldiers of the 9th Cavalry and 38th and 125th Infantry. Today, the fort is open from dawn to dusk, seven days a week. Maintained by the Bureau of Land Management, the site has interpretive signs. There are also hosts provided by the Bureau of Land Management at Fort Craig from April 1 to October 1. Fort Craig is about 35 miles south of Socorro. http://www.blm.gov/nm/st/en/prog/recreation/socorro/fort_craig.html

SUNLAND PARK (SEE ALSO LAS CRUCES)

On the border of Texas and Mexico, Sunland Park is a suburb of both Las Cruces, New Mexico and El Paso, Texas. There's nothing historic about the town, which makes it a bit of an anomaly in New Mexico, but it is a popular destination for two reasons.

The town was actually named for the **Sunland Park Racetrack and Casino**. The combination of racetrack and casino is also known as a racino in the states in which it is legal, and that includes New Mexico. Open since 1959, it is a quarter-horse track with its own Sunland Derby.
1200 Futurity Drive
Sunland Park, NM 88063-9057
(575) 874-5200
http://www.sunland-park.com/

Located across from the racetrack, **Western Playland Amusement Park** caters to families with its over 30 rides. Open seasonally.
1249 Futurity Drive
Sunland Park, NM 88063
(575) 589-3410
http://westernplayland.com/

Sunland is also famous for a more reverent reason—**Mount Cristo Rey**. Sculpted by Urbici Soler and completed in 1939, the 29-foot-tall limestone statue watches over the land below from atop the Sierra de Cristo Rey. There's also an annual pilgrimage held the last Sunday of October. Call for information on events and dates when you can visit Mount Cristo Rey.
(915) 252-9840
(915) 731-0784
http://www.mtcristorey.com/

TRUTH OR CONSEQUENCES (SEE ALSO ELEPHANT BUTTE)

Fondly abbreviated as T or C, the town was known as Hot Springs until a deal came along that it couldn't refuse.

In 1950, Ralph Edwards, the host of the very popular radio quiz show called Truth or Consequences, announced that he would air the program from the first town that renamed itself after the show. Hot Springs jumped on it, changed its name, and Edwards visited newly renamed Truth or Consequences during the first weekend of May, and he did so for the next fifty years. The city still celebrates Fiesta each year on the first weekend of May.
http://www.sierracountynewmexico.info/annual-event/truth-or-consequences-fiesta/
https://www.facebook.com/Truth-or-Consequences-FIESTA-448155115292/

T or C is a popular tourist destination for those who come to soak in the hot springs. The town sits atop a large natural aquifer that produces somewhat salty, odorless water ranging in temperature from 100 to 115 degrees Fahrenheit. With almost 2,700 parts per million of assorted minerals, these thermal springs constitute some of the most heavily mineralized water in the United States. It's also a popular place to stay when visiting nearby Elephant Butte Lake.

Located in the downtown **Hot Springs Bathhouse Historic and Commercial District,** the spas and bathhouses that brought visitors to the town are still open for delicious soaks.

165

You can find more information on these options here: http://www.sierracountynewmexico.info/attractions/truth-or-consequences-hot-springs/

Visitors to **Spaceport** America also start their tours in the T or C visitor center, housed in a 1935 pueblo-style adobe building downtown. New exhibits and hands-on displays highlight the future of space travel. Spaceport America tour operator, Follow the Sun Inc., leads daily guided tours from the visitor center. All tours require a minimum 24-hour advance reservation by phone or online.
301 S Foch St.
Truth or Consequences, NM 87901
(844) 727-7223
http://spaceportamerica.com/experience/

While strolling through downtown Main Street, stop **at Las Palomas Plaza at Geronimo Springs**. Designed by Shel Neymark as a gathering space in the center of town, you'll want to enjoy the flowing hot mineral water of Geronimo Springs. Sit on the carefully placed benches and dip your hands and feet into the water. The two 12-foot-tall ceramic mountains symbolize a place of healing and rejuvenation. Next door, the Geronimo Springs Museum highlights local history.
211 Main St.
Truth or Consequences, NM 87901
(575) 894-6600
http://geronimospringsmuseum.com/

WHITE SANDS MISSILE RANGE MUSEUM (SEE ALSO WHITE SANDS NATIONAL MONUMENT)

The white gypsum dunes that look like brilliantly white sand have given rise to two completely different experiences, and at different ends of this sprawling area. White Sands National Monument offers a playground unlike any other in the world, while White Sands Missile Range was a proving ground for some of the most sophisticated technology produced in the United States. And, just to add a bit more to the confusion, the national monument is technically located in the southeast part of the state while the missile range is technically in the southwest section, which is what happens when lines are arbitrarily drawn.

The White Sands Missile Range is off-limits to visitors, except for the White Sands Missile Range Museum that is right in front. It displays the missiles and rockets that had been tested at this crucial military installation. The museum likes to call the display, which has over 50 pieces of sophisticated military technology, the Missile Park.

Located 22 miles east of Las Cruces and 44 miles west of Alamogordo off Highway 70, there is no cost to visit the museum, but visitors will need to provide their driver's license, vehicle registration, and proof of vehicle insurance before they will be allowed onto the Missile Range. The museum itself has limited hours, but the Missile Park is open seven days a week from dawn to dark.

To find the Missile Range, turn off Highway 70 between markers 169 and 170. There are signs on the highway.
(505) 678-8824
http://www.wsmr-history.org

SOUTHEAST

This is definitely one of the quirky and larger than life parts of the state. Smokey Bear, bats in the cavern, the remains of the most ancient peoples in the area, and (of course) the beloved and baffling extraterrestrials are all highlights of this region of the state.

ALAMOGORDO (SEE ALSO WHITE SANDS MISSILE RANGE)

The main reason to visit Alamogordo is definitely the White Sands National Monument just outside of the city. Alamogordo's other attractions include atomic history, giant nuts, and an amazing display of the Shroud of Turin.

Famous for being the test site of the atomic bomb, it's only possibly to visit **Trinity Site** one weekend twice a year in April and in October. But it is worth a visit. Everyone goes to see the black stone obelisk marking the place where the first atomic bomb was detonated on July 16th, 1945. It is a site of devastation, albeit military importance.

The place of more visual and human interest is the **Schmidt House/McDonald Ranch.** The simple rooms in a 1930s-era farmhouse became the assembly space for a bomb. Ranch buildings, an ice house, as well as that small vintage tin-roofed farmhouse form an image of early ranching life. Visitors can walk through the house and see exhibits and photos from that era.

After the test, which blew out the windows, the house was left empty and slowly deteriorated. In 1982, the US Army stabilized the house, and with the help of the Department of Energy and the National Park Service, restored the building back to its 1945 appearance.

Although not a shred is left from the families who lived there, there is still a sense that people once called it home, before it became the site of the assembly of the first atomic bomb.
http://www.wsmr.army.mil/PAO/Trinity/Pages/Home.aspx
(575) 678-1134

White Sands National Monument is an experience like no other. The pure white dunes stretch across the horizon like a huge sandy desert. But these dunes are not made of sand (or silica). These blindingly white dunes are made of gypsum. Once upon a time the area was covered by the Permian Sea. When it began to dry up, massive deposits of gypsum were left behind.

Gypsum is probably best known for its beautiful form as alabaster, but it's also used to manufacture gypsum board (also known as drywall or plasterboard). The White Sands National Monument in New Mexico is the world's largest gypsum dune field.

The effect is like snow that never melts. In fact, sections of the monument have been set aside as a play area for sledding on the dunes. If you didn't bring your own sled you can buy one at the park and then sell it back at the end of your visit for a portion of the purchase price. What you won't be able to do is construct a sand castle. There's not a bit of moisture in the gypsum to hold it together.

The entrance is located off I-70 about 15 miles south of Alamogordo (and 50 miles north of Las Cruces). http://www.nps.gov/whsa/index.htm

GOING NUTS FOR PISTACHIOS
There are two side-by-side pistachio farms near Alamogordo, and both offer friendly people eager to showcase their pistachios and wine.

It's easy to find **McGinn's Pistachio Tree Ranch**. Just look for the giant pistachio by the side of the road. McGinn's is home to the largest pistachio in the world (made out of concrete, of course), but it is pure roadside fun to stop and take your picture posed by the giant nut. An animatronic farmer explains how pistachios are grown, and you can sample some of the products made at McGinn's such as pistachio brittle and flavored nuts. They also offer a free tour of the groves on a special small bus.

7320 US-54/70
Alamogordo, NM 88310
(575) 437-0602
http://www.pistachioland.com/

Just next door at **Heart of the Desert**, the atmosphere is more sophisticated and the space is bigger. They also offer a free tour and free samples, including pistachio biscotti and pistachio popcorn. If you want to sample some New Mexico wines, Heart of the Desert offers a large and inviting tasting bar.

7288 US-54/70
Alamogordo, NM 88310
http://www.heartofthedesert.com/

Alamogordo is also home to **the New Mexico Museum of Space History** (next to the New Mexico State University—Alamogordo). There are some interesting artifacts, and it's fascinating to see the range of individuals inducted into the International Space Hall of Fame.

You'll also find the burial site of HAM, the first "astrochimp." His name was an acronym for Holloman Aerospace Medical Center, which trained him for the mission. He was successfully launched and recovered on January 31, 1961. After the flight he was sent to live out his remaining years at the National Zoo in Washington, DC and then brought back for burial after his death.

You don't need to pay the admission to see some of the really fun parts—the older pieces of technology. There's also an IMAX theater, but that's a separate charge.

3198 State Route 2001
Alamogordo, NM 88310
(575) 437-2840
http://www.nmspacemuseum.org/

Toy Train Depot is located in the city park but run separately. This tiny depot and train is a fun ride for kids and a museum perfect for train lovers.
1991 N White Sands Blvd.
Alamogordo, NM 88310
(575)437-2855

In a mall that has almost as many empty stores as merchants is one of most unexpected experiences to be found in Alamogordo. **Shroud of Turin** is a storefront museum dedicated to the Shroud of Turin and the scientific evidence in support of the shroud as having once held the body of Jesus. You don't have to be Christian or religious to find this quite a striking and fascinating experience. Staff members are on hand to walk you through the exhibits.
923 New York Ave.
Alamogordo, NM 88310
(575) 415-5206
http://www.shroudnm.com/

Alameda Park Zoo, opened in 1898, covers 12 acres and over 250 exotic and indigenous animals. It is one of about 220 zoos to hold AZA accreditation, and one of only three in New Mexico (the other two are in Albuquerque and Carlsbad).
1321 N White Sands Blvd.
Alamogordo, NM 88310
(575) 439-4290
http://ci.alamogordo.nm.us/coa/communityservices/zoo.htm

ARTESIA

Founded in the 1880s when the promise of water made the area attractive for farming and ranching, the town has answered to several names. The first name was "Miller," which came from an early railroad employee. For a brief time, the town was "Stegman" after the first postmistress, Sallie Chisum Robert Stegman, niece of John Chisum of the Chisum cattle trail fame. Upon her divorce Sallie dropped the "Stegman," perhaps causing a bit of a quandary for the town, but with the discovery of artesian water wells in the area, the fledgling town was soon renamed "Artesia" and officially incorporated in 1905.

Artesia radiates a sense of prosperity, traced directly to the recent oil and gas boom. In fact, a refinery is practically in the middle of the town. Small replicas of the oil rigs sit alongside the railroad tracks by the visitor center. In town, there are at least two buildings with petroleum in the name.

Pedestrian-friendly downtown Artesia is known for its striking bronze sculptures that focus on **Artesia's Old West heritage**. Strolling the streets will lead visitors to most of them, but it's worth picking up a copy of the walking tour and map at the visitor center, or following the links on this page: http://www.artesiachamber.com/vi/index.htm

Local artists have also contributed to Heritage Walkway, colorful murals in downtown Artesia which provide a mini-view of Artesia's history.

The **Artesia Historical Museum and Art Center** offers a variety of art and historical exhibits.
505 W Richardson Ave.
Artesia, NM 88210
http://www.artesianm.gov/154/Museum-Art-Center

The **Visitor Center in the Historic Train Depot** offers a comprehensive glossy guide to the local art. In 1912 the depot was converted to a freight depot, and the current structure was built as a passenger depot.
107 N First St.
Artesia, NM 88211
(575) 746-2744

The library is new, modern, and large. But its artistic highlight is their rescued fresco mural made by Peter Hurd (See San Patricio for the New Mexico connection).

Hurd created **The Future Belongs to Those Who Prepare for It** for Prudential Insurance in 1952, using the centuries-old fresco technique of applying the paint directly onto the plaster. The mural was painted on site in the lobby of the Prudential Insurance Building in Houston, but when the building was scheduled for demolition, private donors stepped forward to save the mural and bring it to Artesia.

205 W Quay
Artesia, NM 88210
(575) 746-4252
http://www.artesianm.gov/146/Library

BLACKDOM

There's nothing left of this particular ghost town except a roadside plaque on Route 285 between Roswell and Artesia just north of Highway 558. But it has an important place in the story of New Mexico.

About 20 miles from Roswell, Blackdom was founded in 1901 by Frank and Ella Boyer under the Homestead Act. Frank's father Henry was a black freeman who served in the military, and Frank grew up with stories of New Mexico. Both Frank and his wife were college-educated teachers, and when they began to challenge the repressive laws of the South, their lives were threatened by the Ku Klux Klan. They decided to move to New Mexico.

Frank decided to build a community that would be free from the limitations and prejudice of the South, and the Homestead Act of 1862 was the means to that goal. The conditions were simple: any adult citizen who had not borne arms against the United States could claim 160 acres of surveyed government land. Claimants only needed to construct a dwelling of some kind and cultivate the land. After five years, that individual could own the land totally and completely (although a small registration fee was required). It was a particular boon to Union soldiers who could actually use their time served in the Army toward that five-year requirement.

Several other places in New Mexico attracted black homesteaders, but Blackdom was the most famous. At its height in 1908 it was home to 25 families and had a population of about 300 people. It was a complete town with a post office, blacksmith shop, stores, a weekly one-page newspaper, and the Blackdom Baptist Church.

Unfortunately, the bright future of Blackdom was cut short by drought—the scourge of farms and ranches throughout the

173

state. The water table began to drop, wells failed, and then so did the crops. The families began to move to other communities. The Boyers eventually moved to Vado, New Mexico, where descendants still live today. By the mid-1920s, Blackdom was vacant.

On October 26, 2002, governor of New Mexico, Gary Johnson, dedicated a historical marker at a rest stop on Highway 285. Although Blackdom has disappeared into history, the New Mexico PBS show, Colores, can recreate just a bit of that era. https://youtu.be/AZO0-8P6hso

You can read more about Blackdom here: https://www.cabq.gov/humanrights/public-information-and-education/diversity-booklets/black-heritage-in-new-mexico/the-town-of-blackdom

CAPITAN

This is Smokey Bear's town, and it radiates a spirit of fun and playfulness. Of course, there are the gift shops and galleries of any tourist town. Fans will want to visit the actual grave of the real Smokey, America's most beloved bear, but the best place to get Smokey's story is in the small cabin next door.

In 1950, a devastating fire swept through New Mexico's Capitan Mountains, and a little bear cub took refuge from the flames high in an oak tree. He was rescued and named Smokey Bear ("the" was inserted later and the alteration stuck).

There's a modern **Smokey Bear Historical Park** where Smokey is actually buried, but you don't have to pay or walk through it to see his grave. It is outside the building with a plaque and sign. Inside, there are exhibits about the dangers of fire but very little about the actual bear.
118 Smokey Bear Blvd.
Capitan, NM 88316
http://www.emnrd.state.nm.us/SFD/SmokeyBear/SmokeyBearPark.html

The **Smokey Bear Museum and Gift Shop** next door is where visitors learn the Smokey fact and fiction. Still in the original log building from when the museum was started, the small space is filled with memorabilia, photos, and people who are eager to tell you Smokey's story, including some behind the scenes information. This is definitely a fun stop.

102 Smokey Bear Blvd.
Capitan, NM 88316
(575)354-2298
http://villageofcapitan.org/museum/museum.html

CARLSBAD

Carlsbad is another oil-fracking town with attractions that go beyond the famous caverns, although Carlsbad Caverns National Park really is enough of a reason to visit.

Carlsbad Caverns National Park 5is actually about 30 minutes away in White City (which is more a convenience stop with souvenir shops, a gas station, and a motel).

Visiting this national park should be done early in the day to allow enough time to wander the paths and be mesmerized by the formations.

There are two ways of getting down into the caverns. The natural entrance to this underground world takes you down a steep but paved path that the park estimates will take about an hour or more. The other way is to take the elevator. The cutoff for using the natural entrance is 2:00 p.m.—so if you arrive after that time, you'll have to take the elevator. The cutoff for the elevator is 3:30.

Guided tours are available and reservations are required, but even without the tour, the caverns are spectacular.

The trail around the perimeter of the huge main room is divided into two parts, and park staff closes off the entrance to the back half at 3:45. Be aware of the time because the formations are astounding, and you may find yourself stopping frequently to admire nature's artistry (or take photos) and then learn that the back half has been closed.

Even so, you'll have plenty to see. The lighting in the cavern is perfect, creating a fairyland of shapes and sizes. You're allowed to use a flash, but these artificially lit photos can't capture the magic of the cavern lighting. Either use a tripod, or balance your camera on the railings for a more extended exposure.

One of the more unusual experiences available at Carlsbad Caverns is their Bat Flights. At sunset, thousands of bats leave the caverns seeking insects. There's a free evening Bat Flight ranger talk available in summer.
727 Carlsbad Caverns Highway
Carlsbad, NM 88220
(575) 785-2232
http://www.nps.gov/cave/index.htm

Carlsbad is also home to one of the few remaining drive-in movie theaters—the **Fiesta Drive-In**, which is open weekends. The sound now comes through the radio and not the speakers that used to be hooked onto your car window. Settle back in the comfort of your car to eat, drink, watch a movie, and make a bit of noise.
401 W Fiesta Drive
Carlsbad, NM 88220
(575) 885-4126
https://www.facebook.com/fiestadrivein

Carlsbad is located at the northern end of the Chihuahuan Desert (which extends downward into Mexico). **The Living Desert Zoo and Gardens State Park** is a surprisingly fun walk through the ecosystems of that desert. Botanical signs include the traditional information, but also explain the functions of the plants for humans —how they used them for food, weaving material, medicinal purposes, and more. Living in a desert, little was wasted.

The facility is also a New Mexico state animal rescue facility, so set amid the sections landscaped to showcase desert environments and plants are spacious fenced-in sections for these animals.
1504 Miehls Rd.
Carlsbad, NM 88220
(575) 887-5516
http://www.emnrd.state.nm.us/SPD/livingdesertstatepark.html

CARRIZOZO (SEE ALSO WHITE OAKS)

The unusual name comes from the Spanish carrizo, meaning reed grass, which grew in the area and was used to feed the ranch cattle. No one knows why an extra "zo" was added—perhaps for emphasis or because it sounded fun.

At first Carrizozo was eclipsed by the mining mecca of White Oaks, but thanks to the railroad, the town of Carrizozo turned the tables, and soon merchants and residents from White Oaks were moving to the new railroad town. It eventually became the Lincoln County seat.

Today, Carrizozo is still the county seat, but there is little to see beyond some shops in the heart of the town. It's more the crossroads of two highways. In New Mexico, an excellent rule for road trips is to keep the gas tank of your car at least half-full, and this part of the state does not have an abundance of gas stations. If you're going to be driving through the area, fill up the car in Carrizozo.

Nearby is the **Valley of Fires Recreation Area** with RV sites and a nature trail. Definitely stick to the trail, as walking on volcanic rock is treacherous.

It is quite amazing to see a huge stream of black volcanic rock suddenly appearing on the horizon. The volcanic rocks are part of the Malpais Lava Flow, dating back approximately 5,000 years.

It's considered to be one of the youngest lava flows in the continental United States. This long, narrow black river of rock is four to six miles wide, 160 feet thick, and covers 125 square miles. It's located four miles west of the Town of Carrizozo on US 380.
http://www.blm.gov/nm/st/en/prog/recreation/roswell/valley_of_fires.html

CLOUDCROFT (SEE ALSO SUNSPOT)

At over 9,000 feet above sea level, this rural mountain town set amid the Lincoln National Forest and the

Sacramento Mountains can literally take your breath away if you're not used to the altitude. But even if you are, this is still breathtaking country. The railroad constructed the town to provide timber for the railroad's own expansion. But the beauty of the area and its mild summers made it an early tourist destination.

Today people still visit the town for the historic **Lodge at Cloudcroft** with its Victorian feel and ghostly legend as well as excellent food. The restaurant, Rebecca's, was named in honor of a beautiful red-haired and once-upon-a-time chambermaid said to haunt the hotel.

If you're a golfer, from April through October you can play golf at the lodge on one of the world's highest courses.

Over the years, the lodge has hosted Judy Garland, Gilbert Roland, Clark Gable, and even Pancho Villa. It is said that Garland and Gable carved their names into the wood of the tower. If you climb up, you can see those names incised in the wood, under a protective glass frame. Both Garland and Gable did stay at the lodge while filming nearby, but that's as far as authentication can go.

601 Corona Place
Cloudcroft, NM 88317
(800) 395-6343
http://www.thelodgeresort.com/

The **Cloudcroft Light Opera Company** offers free summer melodramas in Zenith Park Pavilion.
http://www.cloudcrofttheatre.com/

The Sacramento Mountains Museum & Pioneer Village encompasses two and a half rustic acres with exhibits of the history of Cloudcroft, models of the little railroad, panoramic photographs of the old lodge, and other significant landmarks.
1000 US-82
Cloudcroft, NM 88317
(575) 682-2932
http://cloudcroftmuseum.com/

Hikers will want to head to the **Trestle Recreation Area** located at the west end of the Village of Cloudcroft. It incorporates the Mexican Canyon Railroad Trestle, the largest trestle constructed and still standing today. There are six trails within the Trestle Recreation area ranging from a quarter-mile accessible trail to an eight-mile loop. Trails average an elevation of approximately 8,000 feet, which can make hiking difficult if you're not used to the altitude.

The main facility is a replica of the old Cloudcroft train depot. There's also water, restroom facilities, interpretive information, access to trails, and picnic sites. Located west of the NM130/US82 intersection, turn onto Forest Road.

http://www.fs.usda.gov/recarea/lincoln/recarea/?recid=34242

> ## Did You Know...
>
> ### New Mexico's State Song Is Quite Unusual?
>
> It's actually quite common for states to have an official song. Some have even more than one. But only New Mexico has a state cowboy song: "Under New Mexico Skies." It was written by Syd Masters of Edgewood. Governor Richardson also signed legislation on March 25, 2009 designating a custom guitar by an Albuquerque firm, Pimentel and Sons, as New Mexico's official guitar. The handcrafted guitar known as the New Mexico Sunrise features inlaid Zia sun symbols.
>
> As far as anyone knows, we're still the only one with a state cowboy song, but Ohio has a state rock song. It's "Hang On Sloopy," and it's been official since March 2015.

Cloudcroft is also the beginning of the road that takes visitors to the Solar Observatory in Sunspot.

CLOVIS (SEE ALSO PORTALES)

Not too many people have heard of Clovis, but there are some cool things about this tiny town, including music history, and prehistory.

For starters, it's the home of the Clovis Sound. In the 1950s some of the biggest names in music came to Clovis to record.

Buddy Holly and the Crickets, Roy Orbison, Buddy Knox, Waylon Jennings, and Chita Rivera all traveled to New Mexico to record their music at Norman Petty's 7th Street Studio in Clovis.

Norman Petty was also a musical phenomenon in his own right. Petty, along with his wife Vi and guitarist Jack Vaughn, formed a successful 1950s musical group called the Norman Petty Trio. In 1956, their major hit "Mood Indigo" sold a half million copies and just one year later in 1957, their song "Almost Paradise" hit #18. Although neither of the Pettys is still alive, the **Norman & Vi Petty Rock & Roll Museum** and the 7th Street Studio are important Clovis attractions.

The museum displays artifacts from the studio including the original mixing board used by Norman Petty to record Buddy Holly and the Crickets. Other artifacts include numerous photographs, musical instruments, an extensive radio collection, and other memorabilia. A jukebox plays songs from the '50s. The Museum is open during regular business hours but is closed for lunch. As always, it's wise to check the hours.
105 E Grand Ave.
Clovis, NM 88101
(575) 763-3435
http://www.pettymuseum.com/

The **7th Street Studio** contains original equipment and the furnishings it had in the late '50s when Buddy Holly came to record. Open only for tours that must be booked in advance.
1313 W Seventh St.
Clovis, NM 88101
(575) 763-3435
http://www.clovisnm.org/pages/norman-petty-studios

Clovis is also the home of two historic theaters. The **Lyceum** opened in 1921 as a vaudeville house. It showed its first talkie in 1929 and closed in 1974. It is currently being restored as part of the Main Street program with an opening expected late in 2016.
411 N Main St.
Clovis, NM 88101
(575) 309-8370
https://www.facebook.com/LyceumClovis

The Modernist **State Theater** opened January 3, 1940 with a distinctive huge circular column that was covered in glass brick. Now a privately owned special events venue, it's worth a look for its architecture.
504 N Main St.
Clovis, NM 88101

Built in 1925 to show movies, the **Mesa Theater** later became home to local music legend Norman Petty's radio station and recording studio. LeAnn Rimes recorded her hit "Blue" at the theater in 1994 when she was 12 years old. Owned by Clovis Community College, plans have been in the works to turn it into the Norman and Vi Petty Performing Arts Center.

Clovis was also a railroad town, and the AT&SF built the town's depot in 1907. Today the depot is the **Clovis Model Train Depot Museum** and welcomes visitors and model train enthusiasts. A self-guided tour enables visitors to run nine different model train layouts. Currently open but visitors are advised to call to check hours.
221 W First St.
Clovis, NM 88101
(575) 762-0066
http://www.clovisdepot.com

SPECIAL FOCUS: CLOVIS HUMANS

The history of the people of New Mexico goes back over 12,000 years to a time when the only evidence of their existence came from the artifacts they left behind. In the case of the earliest prehistoric residents, known collectively as Clovis Man, these objects were distinctive projectile points fabricated and found in the area near the town of Clovis.

The discovery of Clovis culture came in 1932 when Edgar B. Howard uncovered a mass of mammoth bones. But it was the narrow, finger-long spear points buried among the bones that caused the excitement. These Clovis points were the tips of the spears used by the area's early humans.

Although first found in Clovis, the points have since been found across all of North America. In terms of archaeological time frames, the tips seemed to have appeared suddenly and spread quickly, perhaps the result of the edge this new design provided for the users. But after 300 or 400 years, the tips disappeared, eclipsed by more efficient and effective designs. The fate of the Clovis people and their culture remains unknown.

Despite the name, the best place to learn about Clovis culture is in Portales, where there is an archaeological dig and museum focused on New Mexico's earliest humans.

FORT SUMNER

Although most famous for being the burial site of famed outlaw of the American West, Billy the Kid, ironically, the exact location of his remains is open to question.

Billy the Kid Museum hosts what the museum considers to be his grave. Although that's open to debate, one thing is quite certain: his headstone has been repeatedly stolen by souvenir hunters. The result is that poor Billy is still behind bars, even in death. There's a metal fence surrounding one of his possible graves.
1435 E Sumner Ave.
Fort Sumner, NM 88119
(575) 355-2380
http://www.billythekidmuseumfortsumner.com

The other, and more likely, contender for Billy the Kid's grave is the Fort Sumner cemetery. But that presents other problems for anyone who wants to visit his final resting place. At the time of his death, no one knew Billy would become so famous that people would make pilgrimages to visit the place of his interment. His grave was likely either unmarked or poorly marked at the time of his death. Bad enough, but then the Pecos River flooded in 1904 and washed away some of the cemetery and the graves, and perhaps Billy's remains as well. Of course, that didn't stop anyone from putting up a memorial headstone—that may or may not be over his grave.

Best advice? If you want to know about Billy the Kid, head to Lincoln. You won't be seeing his grave, but you will understand his life and his death.

182

Navajo Long Walk to Bosque Redondo is now a New Mexico State Monument and Memorial. A museum has been designed by Navajo architect David Sloan. There's an interpretive trail, and information about the tragic history of Fort Sumner and Bosque Redondo Indian Reservation. A permanent exhibit tells the story of the Native people who were forced to move to Bosque Redondo.
3647 Billy the Kid Road
Fort Sumner, NM 88119
http://www.nmmonuments.org/bosque-redondo

SPECIAL FOCUS: THE LONG WALK

Fort Sumner is known for being the site of one of the greatest injustices against the Navajo people—the Navajo Long Walk. Fort Sumner, the center of the Bosque Redondo Indian Reservation, was created as the very flawed solution to the issue of the increasing friction between the government of the United States and the Navajo Nation and the Mescalero Apache.

The Army started by convincing the Mescalero people to move to a new fort being constructed at Bosque Redondo, to be named Fort Sumner. It was to be located far away from any settlements.

The lure for the Mescalero was a new treaty that would at some point give the Mescalero permission to go back to their Native lands. No sooner had they moved then General James H. Carleton, who had initiated the plan, changed his mind. He expected to find lucrative gold and silver mines on both the Apache and Navajo territories which would bring great wealth to the United States. Giving the Mescalero seeds and tools, Carleton anticipated that they would metamorphose from nomadic hunters to farmers. And their lives really did depend on it. It didn't work out that way.

Having convinced the Mescalero to relocate to Fort Sumner, Carleton turned his attention to the Navajos. The Navajo turned down the offer. Growing frustrated, Carleton asked Kit Carson to solve the problem. Carson's solution was the complete destruction of Navajo crops and the killing or capture of their livestock. There was even a bounty paid to soldiers for each horse, mule, and sheep they captured from the Navajos. (See Taos and the controversy over Kit Carson).

183

Finally, the Navajo capitulated. In February 1864, nearly 3,000 Navajos surrendered, and about 2,000 began the infamous forced march known as the Long Walk across New Mexico to Fort Sumner. It was a grueling trek and many died of exposure and hunger along the way. In April, several thousand more undertook the long killing march.

Ultimately, 6,000 Navajos as well as the 400 Apaches were camped at Bosque Redondo. The food was totally inadequate and near-starvation conditions weakened those who survived the forced trek.

The abominable conditions eventually forced a change in public and government sentiment, and in May 1868, four years after the Navajo was force-marched to Bosque Redondo, a treaty was signed and the Mescalero and Navajo were allowed to return to their homelands. For the Navajo, that was the Four Corners area of the state. The treaty also acknowledged Navajo sovereignty, and they are known today as the Navajo Nation.

Read more information at:
http://newmexicohistory.org/people/navajo-long-walk-to-bosque-redondo-1864

For the Native American perspective visit:
http://www.bosqueredondomemorial.com/

For a video on the Long Walk from the Navajo perspective:
https://www.youtube.com/watch?v=F0hGlPvXXKs

FORT STANTON

From military enclave to medical facility, Fort Stanton has seen a lot of history.

In 1855 the farmers along the Bonita River wanted protection from attacks by the Mescalero Apache. The answer, in part, was the establishment of Fort Stanton, which was also another site of the Buffalo Soldiers.

After its military career ended, Fort Stanton became a tuberculosis hospital, then a facility for the care of the mentally challenged, then a women's low-security correctional facility.

Today it has become a New Mexico State Monument and an official Historical Site with the focus on its military past. The beautiful stone Catholic chapel is open, and there is a museum in the visitor center. Visitors are welcomed to walk the grounds and see all the buildings, even if it is only from the outside.

The Bureau of Land Management (BLM) partners with the site to offer hiking trails throughout the area. There are self-guided tours, as well as special events during summer—reenactors from the Civil War and Indian Wars era, demonstrations, and presentations.

The future of this rare piece of military history is precarious. Funding to stabilize the buildings is often in doubt from year to year. But the volunteers of Fort Stanton have done, and continue to do a great service in its preservation.
Billy the Kid Scenic Byway (Highway 380) on Highway 220
(575) 354-034
http://fortstanton.org

HOBBS

Western Heritage Museum and Lea County Cowboy Hall of Fame is the home of the Linam Ranch Museum collection. Virgil Linam and his wife Thelma both had a passion for preserving history. Most of the items in the Linam Ranch Museum were used by Thelma and/or her husband Virgil's family. These include Native American artifacts, pioneer memorabilia, and special keepsakes, most of which relate directly to the area of southeastern New Mexico. An historic Eclipse windmill was erected in front of the Western Heritage Museum. The museum also hosts special exhibits.
1 Thunderbird Circle
Hobbs, NM 88240
(575) 492-2678
http://www.nmjc.edu/museum

HONDO (SEE ALSO SAN PATRICIO)

The dot on the map that is Hondo is also the site of the studio and fabricating space of designer Alice Warder Seely. That is reason enough to visit, but there's even more art in the area. You'll definitely want to head a few miles down the road to San Patricio for the art of two of America's most famous painting families—the Hurds and the Wyeths.

Alice Warder Seely's jewelry is sold in museum gift shops, stores, and galleries around the country, but if you visit her workshop on Highway 70 in Hondo, you can take a tour and see how her beautiful designs are turned into lead-free pewter jewelry. Be warned, you may leave with some of her beautiful creations.
Mile Marker 286, Highway 70
Hondo, NM 88336
(575) 653-4062
http://www.aliceseely.com/

There's more of Seely's artistry in Hondo. A born and raised New Mexican, in 1999 she and her life partner David Hall bought an old cottage in Hondo and some surrounding acreage. This became the basis of their **Hondo Iris Farm and Gallery**, where she displays her textile work. There's jewelry, clothing, textiles, pottery and more.
Mile Marker 284, Highway 70
Hondo, NM 88336
(575) 653-4062
http://www.hondoirisfarm.com/

LINCOLN

The story of Billy the Kid might be said to have rescued this 1800s town from ghost town status. As it happened, however, Lincoln was at the center of the Lincoln County War (1876-1879), the stage on which the saga of Billy the Kid played out. In a cast of colorful and complex characters, Billy captured the country's attention.

Considered to be one of the more violent episodes in New Mexico history, the Lincoln County War started as a battle between cattlemen, and mercantile competition for Army contracts. It escalated into all-out conflict. And just about the whole town is a historic site.

SPECIAL FOCUS: LINCOLN COUNTY WAR AND BILLY THE KID

Born Henry McCarty in New York City around 1859, young Billy moved around the country with his mother, eventually landing in New Mexico. When Billy's mother died in 1874, the family was living in Silver City, New Mexico. Billy was about 14 years old and soon became involved in petty theft, even going to jail for receiving stolen goods.

Escaping jail, he fled to Arizona, but he soon got into more trouble. He was arrested for killing a blacksmith (allegedly in self-defense). Escaping again, Billy came to Lincoln County, back in New Mexico. Billy (then known as William Bonney) was hired as a cowboy on the ranch of John H. Tunstall.

Tunstall was a young British entrepreneur who was attempting to get into the lucrative business of provisioning the United States Army and the Indian reservations. Tunstall was led into the business by a local lawyer Alexander McSween, who knew that Lawrence Murphy, who had held a lock on that business, had become financially weak. In fact, Murphy had become partners with a man named James Dolan in an attempt to resuscitate the business.

This turned out to be a fatal decision for Tunstall. The Murphy Dolan crowd didn't want the competition, and Tunstall was found murdered in February 1878. That event marked the beginning of the Lincoln County War.

The Office of the State Historian of New Mexico sums up the situation: While Billy's role in this "war" has been over the years the subject of romance and legend, the cold fact of the matter is that the Lincoln County War was an ugly battle between two greedy and ambitious groups of unethical entrepreneurs. They in turn were aided by corrupt county and state officials and corrupt US Army officers. http://newmexicohistory.org/people/billy-the-kid

Tunstall's friends (including Billy the Kid) attempted to avenge his death with the murder of Sheriff William Brady. Brady was an ally of James Dolan, the man allied with Murphy who had taken charge of the group's business interests.

The grand jury, attempting perhaps to end the hostilities, indicted members of both groups in Sheriff Brady's death. Included in the roster of those indicted was Billy the Kid.

Chaos really erupted. Troops brought in to quell the disturbances were actually pro-Dolan. The result was the deaths of several Regulators (as Tunstall's friends were now called). Billy, who had a real talent for escaping tight situations, escaped unharmed once again.

The situation getting messier and messier, the President of the United States finally got involved. President Rutherford B. Hayes dismissed the state's governor (rumored to be corrupt) and replaced him with General Lew Wallace, who attempted to bring the lawlessness of Lincoln County to an end.

Although Wallace pardoned several participants in the feud, Billy wasn't one of them. In fact, Wallace issued an arrest warrant for him. Despite his repeated attempts to secure a pardon, Billy remained branded an outlaw. But for his part, Billy was not exactly contrite. He began to receive notoriety from local journalists, who now dubbed him "Billy the Kid" and called him the most important outlaw in New Mexico.

At this point, yet another character entered the scene. Pat Garrett was appointed sheriff and his most important job was to arrest Billy (and the other outlaws). Although Garrett's first attempt was not successful, he soon captured Billy and brought him to jail in Las Vegas (New Mexico). Billy was sentenced to be hanged on May 13, 1881 in Lincoln County.

By now everyone knew of Billy's ability to escape from jail, so he was placed under 24-hour guard. But even that didn't stop Billy from slipping out of his handcuffs, grabbing a gun and killing both guards. A bystander helped him get a horse while the rest of the town watched (likely from fear, as Billy was reported to have threatened anyone who tried to stop him).

Billy headed to Fort Sumner where he had friends, but by sheer bad luck he showed up at their house while Pat Garrett was there. Garrett immediately shot and killed him. Although that ended the life of Billy the Kid, the legend had only begun.

Most recently, interest has been rekindled by the find of a photograph apparently taken at a wedding of one of the Regulators, with Billy the Kid included. A National Geographic special traced the story.

See a clip from it here:
http://channel.nationalgeographic.com/videos/the-sweater-cowboy/

Several of 17 structures and buildings are open year round, and a few more are open seasonally. The buildings are so well-preserved that you can stroll the quiet street (even though it is legally a highway) and feel you are back in the late 1800s in an Old West town.

Start at the Visitor Center and pick up a map, watch the video, and find out what buildings are currently open.

Definitely visit the two-story adobe **courthouse**, which started out as Murphy's mercantile establishment (L.G. Murphy & Co.), then became the headquarters of the Murphy-Dolan gang. The building eventually became the Lincoln County courthouse and the site of the jail where Billy the Kid was incarcerated and then escaped.

The **Tunstall Store**, opened to compete with L.G. Murphy & Co., contains displays of the original 19th-century merchandise in the original shelving and cases.

In addition to the museum buildings, there are shops and public buildings. The historic (and charming) Dolan House built in 1883 is open for breakfast and lunch.

The **Lincoln Historic District** is a National Landmark and a New Mexico State Historic Site located between Capitan and Hondo on Route 380.

An open-air enactment of The Last Escape of Billy the Kid takes place in August. http://billythekidpageant.com http://www.nmmonuments.org/lincoln

LOVING

Located 13 miles south of Carlsbad, the lure of this town is the post office where you can have your Valentine hand-stamped "Loving."

Sweet sentiments aside, the town was actually named for Oliver Loving, a Texas cowman and trail driver. Loving is also known for the summer of 1866 cattle drive along what came to be called the Goodnight-Loving Trail.

Loving was injured in a Comanche attack while on the trail, just making it to Fort Sumner before he died of gangrene. Temporarily buried there, his son Joe Loving and his friend Charles Goodnight moved him to Weatherford, Texas, where he had wished to be buried.

The Goodnight-Loving Trail has gone down in Southwest cattle-driving history, even sparking a song by Utah Phillips about that cattle trail and the life of the cowboys. His song "Goodnight-Loving Trail" became a classic after being recorded by Tom Waits, among others. Here's a link to a lovely tribute version of the song by a singer known on YouTube as Willy Sunday. https://www.youtube.com/watch?v=a_nGIQkjboU

PORTALES (SEE ALSO CLOVIS)

This town of about 11,000 is home to Eastern New Mexico University, which offers two unique experiences—the Jack Williamson Science Fiction Library, and Blackdraw Museum and archaeological Site.

The **Jack Williamson Science Fiction Library** is one of the world's leading collections of science fiction. Anyone who loves SF, or even is intrigued by this unique genre, should add this library to their itinerary. Williamson has long been considered a founding father of twentieth-century science fiction. In fact, another science fiction titan, Ray Bradbury, credited Williamson as a powerful influence on his writing. Williamson published science fiction books and stories from Metal Man in 1928 to Stonehenge Gate in 2005, shortly before he died at age 98.

This very special library started when Williamson, who taught at Eastern New Mexico University, donated part of his collection. It's been growing ever since. The library now includes science fiction books, pulp novels dating back to the early 1900s, manuscripts, correspondence, and photographs.

Not all the books are strictly science fiction. Some are just fascinating. The oldest in the collection dates to 1663. Another of the intriguing items is a collection of poetry written by Rev. George Crabbe in 1812. It's not the poetry that intrigues but the Fore Edge painting. When the pages of the edge of the book are held together, and then bent slightly at an angle, the gold leaf-colored edges transform into a hand-painted scene of what might be old England.

The collection is located on the top floor of the Golden Library.
1500 S Ave. K
Portales, NM 88130
(575) 562-2636
https://www.enmu.edu/academics/library/collections/jwsf.shtml

Blackwater Draw Museum and Archeology Site is considered one of the oldest sites of Clovis humans, dating back to 11,300 to 11,000 radiocarbon years before the present (RCYBP).

Blackwater Locality No 1 is open seasonally and located on US 70. Visitors walk dirt paths, taking one to two hours to complete the loop. The site is a National Historic Landmark and also listed on the National Register of Historic Places.
(575) 356-5235
(575) 562-2202

Many of the objects from the site are displayed several miles away at the Blackwater Draw Museum. These included fluted points, stone and bone weapons and tools. Additional displays interpret how Clovis people likely lived and the kinds of

191

prehistoric creatures lived at the time. The museum is on Highway 70 just north of Route 202.

(575) 356-5235

(575) 562-2202

https://www.enmu.edu/services/museums/blackwater-draw/

Portales is also home to yet another unusual collection. This is a collection of pieces of early technology that wrested power from the wind—windmills.

Bill and Alta Dalley's Amazing Windmill Collection—while that isn't quite its official name, it should be. At one time drivers in suburban Portales often stumbled upon the surprisingly large collection of windmills amassed by Bill and his wife Alta. The collection started in 1980 when Bill was helping a friend salvage the wood of an old homestead. Among the discarded items on the grounds were the parts of an old windmill. Bill decided to salvage those along with the wood. Once he started, he didn't stop. His backyard contained dozens of museum-quality windmills. In 2012, the Dalleys donated the windmills to Roosevelt County, which has moved his entire collection to the County Fairgrounds for permanent display.

109 W First St.

Portales, NM 88130

http://www.portales.com/attractions_daley.htm

See their collection with the New Mexico True video at: https://youtu.be/g9xmG_CtsTI

ROSWELL

Perhaps no part of the United States is more synonymous with UFOs and extraterrestrials than the town of Roswell. But Roswell also offers science history. The Father of Rocketry, Robert Goddard, came to Roswell in 1930 to further his experimentation in rocket propulsion.

The **International UFO Museum/Research Center** in a converted theater is a strange mix of serious reporting, and kitschy large aliens (perfect for that photo op), as well as small aliens encased in glass cylinders—which are less a photo op, and more a rather disturbing exhibit.

Despite a bit of an air of frivolity, there is some intriguing history. Although the Roswell event is often conflated with the equally enigmatic Area 51, the latter is a United States Air Force facility within the Nevada Test and Training Range. However, Area 51 is said to be the final location of alien material and perhaps even bodies recovered from the Roswell incident.

The famed Roswell Incident started in 1947 when a UFO supposedly crashed on a ranch near Roswell. The center carefully lays out the chronology of the event and its aftermath, and the fierce controversy over exactly what happened that evening (See Special Focus: Weather Balloon or Alien Crash—You Decide).

There are also some other thoughtful exhibits, including one examining what is and what isn't UFO material and investigations of objects supposedly found at the site.

The center has amassed cabinets of reference material, declassified documents, old newspaper articles, books, and pamphlets. Anyone who is serious about the study of UFOs would enjoy spending a bit of time in that library.
114 N Main St.
Roswell, NM 88203
(800) 822-3545
http://www.roswellufomuseum.com/

SPECIAL FOCUS: WEATHER BALLOON OR ALIEN CRASH – YOU DECIDE

According to the International UFO Museum, it all started on July 4, 1947 when Mac Brazel, a rancher on the Foster ranch (75 miles NW of Roswell) heard a loud noise, which he reported sounded different from thunder. Two nuns at St. Mary's saw what they had described as an airplane crash. And the tower at the air force base tracked on radar what they described as a descending flash.

Nothing further happened until the next day, when Brazel was riding the ranch and discovered a debris field that he described as being about the size of three football fields. He reportedly picked up a sack of the material.

On July 6, Brazel took the material to Sheriff Wilcox, who called the Intelligence Officer, Major Jesse Marcel at the military base. Marcel decides to investigate; so on July 7, Brazel and Marcel went to the debris site on the ranch. Although Marcel brought some of this debris to his supervisor, Col. Blanchard, he also reported stopping by his house to show the remnants to his son.

But on July 8, Marcel saw what he believed to be an attempt to hide evidence. Marcel had taken some of the debris to Ft. Worth to General Ramey, who reportedly spread the debris on the floor then requested that Marcel step outside. When he returned Marcel reports that the debris had been replaced with remnants of weather balloon.

What of Brazel during this time? He reports being held by the military and requested to modify his story to support the weather balloon explanation.

On July 9, Gen. Ramey issued a press release that there was no saucer and that the whole thing was just a weather balloon. This was in direct refutation of a previous press release that reported that a "flying disc" was recovered.

Mac Brazel was later reported to have said, "I am sure what I found was not any weather observation balloon."
http://www.roswellfiles.com/Witnesses/brazel.htm

Further, it was speculated that a senior intelligence officer like Major Marcel would certainly know the difference between a weather balloon and UFO debris.

Marcel himself spoke with Leonard Nimoy as part of the In Search Of series (aired 1977 to 1982). Marcel talks about his experiences, including handling these foreign materials, and says, "It was not anything from this earth. That I'm quite sure of."
https://www.youtube.com/watch?v=Z349mbaqRds

Later Investigations
A later report by the Government Accounting Office (GAO) sums up the event: Pursuant to a congressional request, GAO provided information on the 1947 weather balloon crash at Roswell Air Field, New Mexico, focusing on: (1) the requirements for reporting

air accidents similar to the Roswell crash; and (2) any government records concerning the Roswell crash.

It notes that although no military service filed a report on the incident, there was no requirement for them to do so at that time. It also notes that some of the records concerning Roswell activities had been destroyed, but there was no information available regarding when or under what authority the records were destroyed, and that only two government records originating in 1947 have been recovered regarding the Roswell incident.

These reports show that a 1947 FBI record noted that the military claimed an object resembling a high-altitude weather balloon with a radar reflector had been recovered near Roswell, and that the 1947 Air Force report noted "the recovery of a flying disc that was later determined by military officials to be a radar-tracking balloon."

http://www.fas.org/sgp/othergov/roswell.html

But neither the story nor the controversy ended there. In 1990, Major Jesse Marcel's son, also known as Jesse Marcel, was interviewed regarding his recollection of the day his father came home with the debris. He described the pieces using terms like "thick foil like aluminum," "very light," "not shiny." Other pieces he said looked like black plastic, perhaps like Bakelite (which was an early form of plastic). He noted that he saw pieces like small I-beams in dull metallic gray. Little of that part of the interview supported the idea that the debris came from a non-Earth object.

But the interview turned quite interesting when Marcel Jr. was asked what he found most unusual about the debris. He said that the inscription found on the inner surface of these pieces of I-beam "appeared to be a type of writing... that was more like geometric shapes ... curved geometric shapes." When asked if his father, a military intelligence officer, thought it was a weather balloon, he asserted that his father "never did believe it was a weather balloon."

https://www.youtube.com/watch?v=PW_s2yeXvLY

There's also history of the non-UFO kind in Roswell. The **Walker Aviation Museum** (inside the airport terminal at Roswell International Air Center) focuses on the history of the

air force base and the missile silos that were around Roswell. Note that this museum currently closes at 3:30 p.m.
1 Jerry Smith Circle
Roswell, NM 88203
(575) 347-6464
http://wafbmuseum.org

Additional attractions include the **Roswell Museum and Art Center** with its focus on superb regional art. Peter Moran's sketches from the 1880s that record Pueblo life; artists Henriette Wyeth and Peter Hurd, with their focus on southeastern New Mexico's Hondo Valley; as well as contemporary artists and special exhibits are among the highlights. Space science enthusiasts will want to note the **Robert H. Goddard Planetarium** on the grounds of the RMAC.
100 W 11th St.
Roswell, NM 88201
(575) 624-6744
http://roswellmuseum.org/

The art of the former artists-in-residence is on view at the **Anderson Museum of Contemporary Art**.
409 East College Blvd.
Roswell, NM 88201
(575) 623-5600
http://roswellamoca.org/

Roswell is also home to something rarely found in the desert, a delightful lake with a beach. **Bottomless Lake State Park** (about 12 miles east of Roswell) is actually a series of lakes (none of them truly bottomless). They were formed when water dissolved the underground salt and gypsum deposits to create caverns. When the roofs collapsed, sinkholes were formed. The sinkholes then filled with water and became the lakes of the park.

The largest and deepest (at 90 feet) is Lea Lake. It is the only one where swimming is permitted. It is also a historic site with a bathhouse and pavilion constructed in the 1930s (during the Great Depression) by the CCC—Civilian Conservation Corp.

What makes Bottomless Lake special (besides the depth of the water) is its sandy beach, RV park, children's playground and picnic areas. During the summer you can rent a paddleboat to explore the lake. There are trails and wildlife-viewing blinds. It's a lovely oasis in the desert.

545 A Bottomless Lakes Road (Highway 380)
Roswell, NM 88201
(575) 624-6058
http://www.emnrd.state.nm.us/SPD/bottomlesslakesstatepark.html

Located on the Pecos River, **Bitter Lake National Wildlife Refuge** is a draw for wildlife enthusiasts who come to watch its birds and dragonflies. There's even a dragonfly festival each September. The Visitor Center and trails are open Monday through Friday.

4200 East Pine Lodge Road
Roswell, NM 88201
(575) 622-6755
http://www.friendsofbitterlake.com/

Finally, RVers, motorcyclists, and off-road drivers will want to take note of **Mescalero Sands North Dune OHV Area**. Administered by the Bureau of Land Management, this off-roaders delight about 45 minutes from Roswell offers 610 acres of towering 90+ foot sand dunes to explore in high-powered fun. Important note: Bring your own water. The area does have restrooms but no drinking water.

(575) 627-0272
http://www.blm.gov/nm/st/en/prog/recreation/roswell/mescalero_san ds.html

RUIDOSO/RUIDOSO DOWNS (SEE ALSO CAPITAN)

The cities of Ruidoso Downs, Hollywood, Mescalero, and Alto are suburbs of Ruidoso.

While thoroughbred racing dominates horse racing along the East and West Coasts, the Southwest and the heartland of the United States is quarter horse territory. The American Quarter Horse derived its name from its ability to outdistance other breeds in races of a quarter mile or less; some horses have been clocked at speeds up to 55 mph.

Ruidoso Downs Race Track is home to the most prestigious and richest prize in quarter horse racing, the American

Futurity for two-year-old quarter horses, and the museum honoring these impressive and elegant horses. Located on the second floor next door to the administrative offices, the **museum** is, in theory, open all year and not just during racing season, but visitors during the off-season should call to make sure someone will be there to open it.

If you're a racing fan, it is definitely worth that effort to learn more about the horses as well as their jockeys, breeders, owners, and trainers. There's an interactive kiosk that lets you explore early videos, facts, and stories. A display is dedicated to the females of racing—fillies and female riders. Mine That Bird has a mention as well. Although not a quarter horse, this stakes-winning gelding was trained in New Mexico and beat the odds to become a winner. Mine That Bird was 50 to 1 when he reached the starting gate of the 2009 Kentucky Derby. Not only did he win the race, he crossed the finish line almost seven lengths ahead of the rest of the field.

26225 US-70
Ruidoso Downs, NM 88346
(575) 378-4431
http://www.raceruidoso.com/

Many of the objects in the **Hubbard Museum of the American West** came from the collection of Anne C. Stradling and introduce visitors to the culture and people of the West. There's an excellent display of historic wagons that includes one associated with Billy the Kid. The exhibit on underground mining features a mockup of the mine entrance with the board of tags miners used to take with them when they went down to blast the ore out of the earth. A tag missing from the board meant the miner was still underground.

One of the major highlights of the museum is outdoors on its grounds. The sculptural tableau Free Spirits at Noisy Water was created by Dave McGary. A series of eight larger-than-life sculptural metal horses representing the major breeds prance and leap across a grassy hill. These huge and majestic creatures are caught in mid-stride.

26301 Highway 70 West
Ruidoso Downs, NM 88346
(575) 378-4142
http://www.hubbardmuseum.org

Spencer Theater for the Performing Arts is a sleekly designed venue for year-round performances in theater, music, and dance in the nearby town of Alto, New Mexico (about 10 miles out of Ruidoso). Designed by internationally acclaimed Albuquerque-based architect, Antoine Predock, the building embraces the beauty of glass with a sophisticated Crystal Lobby filled with the blown glass art of Dale Chihuly. In fact, the Spencer Theater houses the largest private collection in the Southwest open to public viewing. They offer free tours but reservations are required.

108 Spencer Drive
Alto, NM 88312
(888) 818-7872
(575) 336-4800
http://spencertheater.com/index.html

The final thing to do in Ruidoso is to buy a wooden bear. They are sold throughout the city, especially along Highway 70. The carvers haul away fallen trees and then use chainsaws to carve them into every size bear, with and without cutesy signs.

SAN PATRICIO (SEE ALSO HONDO)

This lush valley hamlet tucked behind Highway 70 alongside the Rio Ruidoso was originally called Libertad (Liberty) by the early Hispanic settlers. La Iglesia de San Patricio, built in 1875, inspired the town to change its name to San Patricio. Peaceful and bucolic now, it was once part of the Lincoln County Wars (made famous because of its connection with Billy the Kid). The town is also the site of a love story between two famous families of artists.

Peter Hurd (1904-1984) was born in Roswell, New Mexico and met NC Wyeth's daughter Henriette (1907-1997) while studying with her father in Pennsylvania. They fell in love, married, and in 1939 they moved back to New Mexico, where their son Michael was born in 1946.

This area remains his home, and the unexpected **Hurd La Rinconada Gallery** features some of the works of the Wyeth and Hurd family artists. Should you feel inspired by the beauty of the valley (or are looking for lodging that isn't in Roswell or

Ruidoso), there are five unique New Mexican-style casitas on the grounds.
105 La Rinconada Lane
San Patricio, NM 88348
(575) 653-4331
(800) 658-6912
http://www.wyethartists.com/

SUNSPOT (SEE ALSO CLOUDCROFT)

Sunspot is little more than a post office, but it's the home of the **National Solar Observatory**. Located in the Lincoln National Forest, you can reach it by a woodsy half-hour ride from Cloudcroft. In summer the Sunspot Astronomy & Visitor's Center offers lectures and free guided tours of the buildings. But you can pick up a self-guided tour booklet at the Visitor's Center even when the tours are not available. The booklets are also available in a box at the beginning of the trail. If you plan to come in winter, call ahead to make sure the facility is open.

The highlight of the tour is the 136-foot-tall Dunn Solar Telescope. Despite its height, there's even more of the building below ground. This is an active site and visitors might well see the staff at work. However, there are no lights or flash photography permitted. Depending on the weather, there's a scenic overlook for a view of the valley, but the 136-foot building itself makes a great photo.

The route to the observatory is the Sunspot Scenic Byway (NM 6563). It is scenic, but there's a bit of added fun along the way. You can see signs naming the planets of our solar system.

Scenic Byway 6563 is about 16 miles south of Cloudcroft (on NM 82) and 40 miles southeast of Alamogordo (on NM 70 and 54) in the village of Sunspot.
3004 Telescope Loop
Sunspot, NM 88349
(575) 434-7000
http://nsosp.nso.edu/visit

TULAROSA

The town and the basin derive their names from the Spanish description for the red- or rose-colored reeds growing along the riverbanks. Although this small town is now more of a suburb of nearby Alamogordo, the area has one major attraction that makes it a must-stop destination.

Three Rivers Petroglyphs is one of the best sites for petroglyphs in the state. It's the largest petroglyph site in the Southwest, in terms of the number of these mysterious carvings—with an estimated 21,000 glyphs. Not only will visitors see these designs along the well-maintained path, but careful exploration is encouraged to see even more.

Visitors will have to climb up steps, but the trail is easy to follow, and has numbered signs to point out some of the highlights, which are keyed to a handout available at the visitor center. A path the other way leads to excavated pit houses, but mainly just the footprints of those buildings remain.

Some of the engravings are so beautifully executed that they seem very much like art, while others designs are clearly stylized symbols. But their locations seem random. Why pick that boulder? What relationship did it have to the other designs two or three boulders away?

In a land of mystery, these creations of the group known as the Jornada Mogollon remain even more tantalizing with their uncertain meanings and purposes.

Located 17 miles north of Tularosa just off US 54, there is a sign for the turnoff, but it fails to mention the petroglyph part of the site. It's right by the Three Rivers Trading Post (which is also worth a visit).
Tularosa, NM 88352
(575) 525-4300
http://www.blm.gov/nm/st/en/prog/recreation/las_cruces/three_rivers.html

WHITE OAKS

It was 1869 when gold was discovered and White Oaks began its ascent. At one time it was the largest town in Lincoln County. Today it might be a ghost of its former self, but this town is not yet dead. It has a functioning church and houses scattered throughout the area. Tourists come to drink in the No Scum Allowed bar. There might also be some historic buildings open as well.

White Oaks is not really near anything, but it's easily reached by taking A044 off Route 54, going north from Carrizozo.

If you close your eyes and imagine, you can see a road lined with small houses and a few other buildings. White Oaks abides.

ONLINE INFORMATION

FESTIVALS

New Mexicans love a good festival. Actually, we're probably always ready to find a reason to eat and celebrate. You can find a complete listing of these events arranged by theme at http://www.newmexico.org/big-annual-events/

For Albuquerque events:
http://www.visitalbuquerque.org/abq365/events/

For Santa Fe events: http://santafe.org/Visiting_Santa_Fe/Must-See_Events/

PUEBLOS

The people of the Pueblos are now primarily located in New Mexico, although at one time their territory stretched into Colorado and Arizona. Their history and culture reach back centuries. The pueblos differ in the opportunities they make available for visitors. In the previous pages of this book, we included the pueblos that are particularly welcoming to visitors; however, many of the smaller groups are open on feast days and special events throughout the year.

You can find a complete listing and brief introduction to the nineteen pueblos of New Mexico at the Indian Pueblo Cultural Center. This is a tribally owned and operated nonprofit consortium. Located in Albuquerque, it's a great place to visit and learn more, as well as enjoy a Native American-inspired lunch or dinner. Their website provides a complete listing of the pueblos and visitor information:
http://indianpueblo.org/19pueblos/index.html

NEW MEXICO FEDERAL AND STATE PARKS

In addition to the national parks included in the pages above, here's a listing courtesy of the National Parks and Monuments in New Mexico http://www.nps.gov/state/nm/index.htm

New Mexico has its own designated state parks. Although some are described in the above pages, use this link to access an interactive map of all the state parks of New Mexico. http://www.emnrd.state.nm.us/SPD/FindaPark.html

Another source for information on the wide open spaces of New Mexico is the Bureau of Land Management. As its name suggests, this government office manages undeveloped government land in New Mexico, and there is a lot of it. New Mexico has 13.5 million acres of public lands, including historical and recreational sites. Learn more about recreational activities at http://www.blm.gov/nm/st/en/prog/recreation.html

The newest national monument in New Mexico is the Organ Mountains-Desert Peaks National Monument. It's administered by the Bureau of Land Management, and you can learn more about it here:
http://www.blm.gov/publish/content/nm/en/prog/NLCS/OMDP_NM.html

Neala McCarten has led a life marked by detours, starting one place, and ending up somewhere unexpected. Born in New York City and raised in Queens, Neala eventually obtained a Ph.D. in Psychology from the State University of New York at Stony Brook.

For the next few years, she wandered through a series of jobs, including that of mother and freelance writer on health and child development. But when her husband died suddenly she needed to reinvent herself and her life.

Asking, "Who would I be if I didn't know who I am?", she finally decided that she was, at heart, a travel writer who lived in Albuquerque, New Mexico. In 2006 Neala quit her job, sold her house in the suburbs, said goodbye to friends and family, and headed to the Land of Enchantment. In 2012 she married James McCarten.

Today, Neala (Schwartzberg) McCarten is the publisher and editor of OffbeatTravel.com, a freelance writer, and a fine art photographer who regularly exhibits in shows in Albuquerque.

Offbeat New Mexico: Places of Unexpected History, Art, and Culture is her first book, dedicated to the state she loves. Perhaps other books will follow. One never knows with life.

30356046R00114

Made in the USA
Lexington, KY
08 February 2019